CONGRATULATIONS, YOU HAVE JUST MET THE CASUALS

CONGRATULATIONS, YOU HAVE JUST MET THE CASUALS

DAN RIVERS

JOHN BLAKE

Published by John Blake Publishing Ltd,
3, Bramber Court, 2 Bramber Road,
London W14 9PB, England

www.blake.co.uk

First published in hardback in 2005

ISBN 1 84454 104 5

British Library Cataloguing-in-Publication Data:

A catalogue record for this book is available from the British Library.

Design by www.envydesign.co.uk

Printed in Great Britain by Creative Print and Design (Wales)

1 3 5 7 9 10 8 6 4 2

Papers used by John Blake Publishing are natural, recyclable
products made from wood grown in sustainable forests.
The manufacturing processes conform to the environmental
regulations of the country of origin.

Photographs © Mirrorpix and *The Courier*, Dundee,
DC Thomson & Co, Ltd.

Foreword

The 1980s saw the birth of the casual scene on the streets and on the football terraces of the United Kingdom. In Scotland in particular a new brand of well-dressed football hooligan appeared, way ahead of many English football crews. The founders of the casual movement in Scotland, the Aberdeen Soccer Casuals (ASC), became the most notorious, feared and copied mob in the country.

This book is not meant to be 'the word' of the ASC nor a definitive version of events. It is just one lad's experiences and observations while involved with the ASC between the Scottish Cup campaign of 1983 and the Skol Cup final in 1989. The original notes I took throughout that period are the main source of the accounts contained within this book. The rest comes from my memories of the time with the benefit of hindsight and a bit more life experience. All of the events in this book did happen and, in as much as is possible, are accurate to the day, but I have used no names as I felt that true Aberdeen lads would know their part in any of the experiences that have been described.

The publication of this book marks the 25th anniversary of the founding of the casual movement in Scotland by the original members of the ASC. Since that turning point in terrace culture, the scene in Scotland has undergone many dramatic changes, and not just with regard to the ever-evolving fashions and the labels and styles attached to them. The scene as I knew it seemed to play itself out at the latter end of the 1980s, and with the advent of rave culture and the arrival of 'E' everything changed. Nevertheless, casual culture is about progression, and the movement came out of the other side, albeit in smaller numbers, and is still alive and kicking today as we've moved into a new century. I wonder how many of them, the originals, have sat back, taken a good look at the scene that they aspired to create, and thought to themselves, Fucking hell, we did this!

The base content of the diary accounts contained within this manuscript was taken from original notes, written between the winter of 1982 and autumn of 1989. Everything described in these pages did happen as stated and, to the best of my recollections, is exactly as it was in the 1980s. I will state now, however, that in some instances, the before- and after-match incidents may have happened the other way round. With the benefit of hindsight and a bit more life experience, all other content has been written in the form of a 'flashback' diary account.

This is just one lad's take on those crazy days as a casual and should not be compared with *Bloody Casuals*, the original ASC book by Jay Allen, which was a masterpiece and way before its time. That book set a precedent for future hooligan biographies. It also inspired me to put all those little bits of paper, diary accounts and memories together to give my own interpretation of what being part of the ASC was about. I would like to take this opportunity to say 'cheers' to those founder members and old-school Aberdeen Soccer Casuals for giving me a mad youth worthy of writing a book about!

Happy anniversary, boys!

Foreword

There are a fair few people that deserve a mention here and I will do my very level best not to leave anybody out.

To John Blake for publishing my work, Lucian Randall at John Blake and Alex Perry for his work on the edit. To the main man 'M' at Casual Culture (you know who you are) for your staunch support since the start of this project and for putting a web page together for me to plug the book and for making me admin and moderator to the site. To Terrace Youth (Fox SYC) for being the first lad on the CC board to offer support and good wishes. To Scooby Doo for always believing in me and backing me through the dance scene and beyond, and for being my best mate. To

DAN RIVERS

Adrian (Mr C) for those days of taking care of me and other lads when it came on top, and for helping me back on my feet when I went haywire. To the two 'Reds' (the trainer and the tree) for your support and many years of friendship. A surprise each, for you boys. To Dougie and Jon for their good wishes. To Stewart for this year's logos, book inserts/cover centre etc and also to the members of the Real Deal, R&R! To the lads from other firms who offered their good wishes and support. To Allen for your faith and backing with the React Tour in 1997 and Greg at FTOF Org and Gorleston Library staff. To ncfc – cheers and respect.

This book is about my time with Aberdeen Soccer Casuals, so the biggest mention has to go to all you lads, past and present, but especially to the lads from those crazy days. To all the senior chaps who started the ball rolling by founding the casual movement in Scotland and for making a name of legend. To all the lads I shared time with in the 1980s, from the trendies back in school days to all the lads I met and stood beside, both at home and on many days out, travelling across the country to support our beloved club and uphold our name.

Finally, to those lads who are no longer with us. Your loss is of great sadness to us all but your names will always be remembered. RIP.

I am especially sad that I didn't get the chance to share this book with my friend who passed away in 2004. You featured in so many of the diary accounts in this book. Surely one of the top lads of my time, Moog, RIP, mate.

Contents

Chapter 1

HOW IT ALL BEGAN

THE CASUALS

So what was it all about for me? Well, it was about being part of a new movement. It was about a new style. It was about the way you dressed and being 'trendy', so as to stand out from the crowd. It was a style with attitude, and as much about the look as it was about any attachment to football.

The 1980s were a fucked-up time in Aberdeen – particularly when it came to fashion. It was all over the place. There was the mod, scooterist and Northern Soul scene, governed by the obvious related clothing of the time. The mods had their Parkas, usually from the army surplus stores and normally US Army issue. There was a shop called One Up that a guy named Fred opened on

2

George Street in the earlier part of the 1980s. I was the very first customer to walk through their door and that was the place to get your clothes if you were into the whole mod thing. They had cycling tops, boating blazers, jam shoes and the like. They also sold bowling shoes, although technically these could be traded at the bowling alley on George Street by popping in with a pair of tatty trainers, playing your set and then slipping out of the door with the shoes still on your feet. Some lads simply went in, paid, got their shoes, and then went to the toilet and did one, pretty much straight away. I know many a lad who went down that route to get those elusive red, white and blue bowling shoes! There was quite a roaring trade in them at one point, and a local cobbler was only too happy to put a sole on them for you.

The scooterists went for a similar military-related style to the mods. Typically, they opted for the MA1 flight jackets and NBC pullover jackets with a hood and patch pocket on the front. A few of the lads I knew wore leather jackets of some description, simply because of the wind-chill factor riding their scooters on the road. Camouflage trousers were also part of the look. A lot of the mods and scooterists were also into their Northern Soul. The soul boys themselves didn't have a uniform as such but were recognisable all the same. A lot of lads in the ASC originally came from a mod, scooterist or soul-boy background.

In the early part of the decade there were also a lot of people who were into the new romantic and poser fashion. What you might call the Haircut One Hundred look. They wore slip-on shoes and tight, shiny trousers with those 'Y' cardigans. They were the white-sock brigade. Oh, and let's not forget the skinhead, punk and 'plastic smelly' (fake biker) scene. The skins were very clean-cut lads, who kept their hair an exact length as part of their culture. They usually sported Harringtons or MA1 flight jackets, and, like the mods, had a lot of union flags and colours in their uniform. Unlike the other fashion groups, who had black Dr Martens shoes or boots as part of their look, the skins wore brown DMs, which were always polished.

The punks had their own look entirely and this was also well catered for at One Up. Some sported spiked Mohawk hair-dos, usually dyed one colour or another. Most had piercings of one sort or another on display. Some wore bondage trousers or skin-tight tartan trousers and most wore DMs. They would also have a lot of Sex Pistols and Exploited merchandise and badges on display. The plastic smelly lot wore leather jackets with skin-tight jeans, usually something like 51 States, and the obligatory DMs or those hideous big-tongued white trainers. They would wear Iron Maiden patches and badges, and I never quite understood where they were coming from, as none of them had motorbikes. They were certainly not part of any bona fide bike culture that I was aware of. Anyway, such were my fashion observations and recollections of the time.

At the start of the 1980s, Aberdeen was the oil capital of Britain and had been described as the 'gateway to the future'. Aberdeen Football Club were on the up too. They had broken the Old Firm's stranglehold on the league by achieving the near-impossible task of going to Celtic Park, Glasgow, home of their closest league challengers and securing a double win in the month of April 1980. That had clinched the Scottish Premier League title and earned them a crack at the highest level of European club football. The prospect of fixtures in England and abroad opened the floodgates for suggestion and change. Suddenly there was a big sportswear boom, and getting 'dressed' for the football, rather than wearing club colours, became the vogue.

Some people point to the meeting between Aberdeen and Liverpool in the European Cup at Pittodrie in October 1980 as the catalyst which launched the Scottish 'casual' scene. On that day, a section of the away support were seen dressed in 'trendy' sportswear – designer tracksuits and top of the range trainers – rather than the traditional club supporter's uniform, which was normal clothing adorned with the team's colours of red and white. These supporters were known as 'Christmas trees' and formed the bulk of the away support.

Some Aberdeen lads had also observed the changeover when going to games in London, and so the founder members of what was to become the Aberdeen Soccer Casuals adopted their own take on the new style and the casual scene in Scotland was born. Lads started travelling down south to the smarter clothing boutiques and sports shops in London. There were also visits to Liverpool and Manchester to keep an eye on the latest looks, while

Edinburgh had stores like Austin Reed, which sold clothes affiliated to the new scene, and the Woollen Mill shop, which sold Burberry. Seeking out the labels and styles in this way was part of what being a trendy was all about, and Aberdeen were the first and founding crew in Scotland to fly the flag of change. The reputation for violence, which was highly sensationalised, came later, but I suppose it was part and parcel of who we were to become.

Fair enough, the battle was important. The confrontation. The chants. The charges. Steaming in. The exhilaration is impossible to describe to people who haven't felt that buzz for themselves. Fear and anticipation meets the rage that comes with the fight for survival. It really is one of those 'you had to be there' feelings! But, for me, being a part of Aberdeen's mob and being a regular face in the crew was the best buzz. Whether you were 50- or 500-strong, this was the ASC. These were your boys: the ones that would watch your back no matter what. We were a unit and we were famous for it, and, yes, we buzzed from it! Fuck all the overhyped and frenzied media attention: 'Aberdeen this' and 'casuals that' and all the bullshit about being mindless thugs. There was fuck-all mindless about Aberdeen. At the core, there was a nucleus of precise organisation – for the most part anyway.

Another important thing about our crew was that we didn't have just one main general. There were the top boys – the older lads – and they made the plans. These plans would then filter down to the necessary faces. Then, by the time match day came around, everybody knew where they had to be and what they had to do. Unfortunately, every mob has got a few 'keeners' – loose cannons that just have to do things their own way. And they always draw the wrong sort of attention. Smashing up property or terrorising innocents was never our gambit. We were there, plain and simple, to support Aberdeen and to fight the other team's mob if they wanted it. Nothing else. Saying that, if you've got a couple of hundred big mealers with scarves on running at you and pelting you with missiles or hitting your fans willy-nilly, you are going to respond. For years as a young Dons fan, many of my fondest football memories were sullied by the abuse that opposition fans dished out time and time again. Whether we beat them or not, it didn't really matter when you went away. I've been on official supporters' club coaches that were stoned and attacked. I've been assaulted and spat at, along with female and family supporters, and generally abused and threatened.

I loved Aberdeen Football Club and I always will. I went to practically every match, home and away. That never stopped. Becoming a casual didn't make me any less of an Aberdeen supporter. Neither did it make me more deserving of a hiding. Some of the media items at the time would have you believe that the casuals deserved everything they got. It was as if we were the only ones dishing out the violence, and people conveniently forgot the years of terror and abuse that we experienced. Not only was it sheer prejudice that made people suggest such

DAN RIVERS

a thing and far too overplayed, but it was also out-and-out ignorance. Like it or not, the fact is that most casuals were staunch and loyal supporters of both club and country, and that goes nationwide. It is a culture unto its own, where dress meets the terrace, and I became absorbed by this culture and embraced it. It's as simple as that!

Chapter 2

'JUST FOR THE FUN OF IT!'

THE CASUALS

It is a fact, and indeed only right to say, that Aberdeen Football Club were Scotland's team of the decade for their achievements in domestic and European football in the 1980s. But 1983 was a particularly amazing year for the players and staff at the club and the supporters alike. That was the year that Aberdeen let the entire world of football know that they were a force to be reckoned with. Along the way they chalked up a historic victory against the mighty Bayern Munich at Pittodrie in a Cup Winners' Cup run that saw Aberdeen destroy Belgian side Waterschei in the semi-final and defeat the favourites Real Madrid in the final in Gothenburg, Sweden.

I can still remember it like it was yesterday. It was

damp and musty but there was an electric atmosphere in a stadium witnessing its biggest ever spectacle. The noise at Pittodrie back then was unbelievable. Absolutely deafening. Everybody to a man would just go completely crazy when we scored. And it doesn't get much better than beating Bayern Munich in your own back yard if you like going loopy. It started with Neil Simpson's equaliser after the Bayern opener had put us on the back foot. There was a heart-stopper of a moment when they went ahead again, which dampened spirits a wee bit once more. But then came that special dummy free-kick between John McMaster and Gordon Strachan and that header from Alex McLeish. The third goal, though, probably lifted the roof off every house in a five-mile radius. For sure they would have heard the crowd noise. I know I bounced from my seat at the front right of the Paddock clean on to the track! I've never known a noise like it. After only being on the pitch for two minutes, super sub John Hewitt scored a peach of a nutmeg off Eric Black's parried effort with only 13 minutes to go. What a night that was. Never to be forgotten!

Then came the 5–1 thrashing of our Belgian opponents in the semi-final at home, setting us up for that most memorable day in Gothenburg when Hewitt's goal gave us victory over the mighty Spanish champions in the final. Those are days that will live and be recounted to generations of fans for ever and ever! There was an amazing belief about Aberdeen at the time and that rubbed off on the people in the city. We felt confident and invincible. Maybe even a bit cocky. Within ten days, we witnessed a Scottish Cup victory against Rangers at Hampden to complete the most amazing season. Aberdeen would cap that by being crowned the top team in Europe with a 2–0 victory over the European Cup winners SV Hamburg, in the Super Cup final second leg at Pittodrie.

Meanwhile, out on the terraces, the Aberdeen Soccer Casuals had grown in confidence and in numbers too and had been going about things their own way to make sure that everybody knew that Aberdeen also had Scotland's number-one mob. After noticing them while working at Pittodrie as a catering assistant with Kenny's catering services in the 1982/83 season, I soon became fascinated and intrigued with their behaviour and dress. I was just 15 and they made a huge impression on me. They were unlike anything I had ever seen before. One of the first things I noticed was the absence of club colours. And, unlike any other fans frequenting the stadium at the time, these lads were turned out sharp in dress, like they were dressed up for something special. Sporting bright pastel-coloured lambswool jumpers and designer-label tracksuit tops. They were a style unto themselves!

There was also an attitude about them. They were bold and confident. They used to have a singsong among themselves and just take the piss. Everything seemed like a laugh to them. It was fun being a casual. They used to sway and point aggressively while getting behind their team, in a manner that I'd only ever witnessed at Anfield, and they were not afraid of using the same manner against the other team's fans. At the same time these lads could be seen 'piston punching' the air with each fist alternately, while having a singsong to 'Come On Eileen' by Dexy's Midnight Runners. I just thought they were fucking excellent. They looked smart and truly didn't give a fuck about being different, or about anything or anyone else.

As a teenager, I liked my football, my clothes and my music. My cousin was my music guru, taking me on various different musical trips, and he was bang into Northern Soul around 1983. There were mods and soul boys where I lived in Portlethen, so I suppose in my search for an identity I used to dress somewhere between the mod style and that of the soul boy, if that's at all possible to understand. I went to two different Academies in that year, Kincorth and Mackie, and hated it more than my time at Dyce prior to that. It was while I was at these two Academies that I came into contact with members of the Aberdeen Casuals. At Kincorth there was this one lad in particular who used to rib me all the time in quite a humorous way. 'Mods are out of fashion!' he used to chant at me. Him and the other trendies, as they called themselves, used to arse about like the lads I'd seen at the football and play fight, slapping each other and chanting 'come on, Aberdeen' and 'we are the Aberdeen soccer trendies'. Just like the lads at the football, they were having a laugh. Doing things for the fun of it. That would serve to become one of my sayings in years to come. Whenever asked why I became an Aberdeen Casual, I

13

would simply reply, 'For the fun of it!' That was reason enough. If it was good enough for these lads, then it was good enough for me.

So, in 1983, I set about joining these smug, well-dressed youths in their Barbour jackets, Pringle jumpers and Lois cords. I grew my side-parting hairstyle until I had a defined and heavy 'wedge', and in the coming year I added a bit of a step to it. My shoes and clothes collection grew and so did my confidence. I would start seeking out the mob in the grounds at home and away to join in their antics, travelling with supporters' club buses at first and later joining the lads on the train. A move from Portlethen to Inverurie at the end of the year saw a new start with new people. The Academy was a relaxed, no-uniform affair and had a good little team of well-dressed lads that did the football. It was through these lads that I would meet more senior members of Aberdeen's mob and start showing my face at known haunts. By the time I left school, after completing my Highers, I had been an Aberdeen Casual for three years. The rest, as they say, is history!

Chapter 3

ABOUT MOTHERWELL

THE CASUALS

It is fairly well documented that after Aberdeen the next team in Scotland to have a crew of trendies turn out on a match day was Motherwell and their Saturday Service (SS). I don't know how the fuck this came about, considering the size of the club and its proximity to the two Old Firm teams who had arguably the largest followings in the whole country, but, sure enough, after many previous encounters involving their skins, here was a new crew of lads, wearing Pringle jumpers and bleached jeans, daring to give it face! A huge fucking feud started over the founding of the casual movement in Scotland and who was the trendiest and hardest mob. Every team had their boys, our Saturday-afternoon

16

adversaries, but this was different. These cheeky chappies from Motherwell had made a challenge to Aberdeen's credibility and position in the trendy stakes and the war with the Saturday Service was to become a special feature on our battle calendar.

By the time I had got it together to do a trip to Motherwell, Aberdeen had already been down and given a good account against their mob. On that occasion, there was a crew of some 120-plus Aberdeen down to Fir Park to do battle. While the majority of Aberdeen fans made their way round to the visitors' gates on the terrace, some 50 or so ASC paid in and made their way up the steps of the Motherwell end and steamed straight towards the back end of the home fans enclosure taunting, 'Come on then, Motherwell, come and have a go,' with loads of people spilling onto the pitch as Aberdeen battled hard with the home mob. The Old Bill (OB) were totally unprepared for the speed and ferocity of this flash-fighting incident but soon moved in and tried to restore some sort of order so that the game could kick off. The Aberdeen mob taunted Motherwell in jubilant fashion during the drawn game, keeping the edgy unrest. The after-match scenario was kept subdued by the back-up that the OB had called in after the start of the game. There was some chanting and missile throwing and a few breakaway charges near a shopping centre, but to my knowledge that was pretty much it. From an Aberdeen Casuals perspective, it had been a good 'day out' and a definite result in our favour. Back in Glasgow, there was some aggro with some Tims (Celtic fans), and as usual some of the lads got off at Dundee to give the Jutes a scare. There were 15 arrests in total and three people were taken to hospital, with one Aberdeen lad suffering a broken leg.

The next time out at Fir Park there was absolute fucking pandemonium. I wasn't privy to the train info on this one and, being a young lad 'oot the road' had to go down on a supporters' bus again. I can only relay what I saw that day and fill in the gaps with what I was told. I do know that the police were far more organised than the last time the two teams met and were on the case of the Aberdeen mob from the minute they hit Glasgow. A half-hour train journey later, they were met by a tidy show of OB, ready to escort them all the way to the ground. There had been some banter exchanged with Motherwell's younger boys, the Tufty Club, as they were becoming known, and some coins were thrown. A few of the boys started taunting 'come on then' but laughing it up as they approached Fir Park. From what I could gather on entering the ground, it was clear to see that Aberdeen had a bigger crew of lads down than had been talked about on the last time out here, with our own younger lads, the Under Fives, numbering nearly 50.

Aberdeen started singing and surging as the game kicked off, upsetting the OB big time. You could feel the rivalry between the two mobs after the way it had all gone off the previous year. The temperature was set to boiling point! There was even more tension between the local OB and us. They hated us. Hated us for being there. For being 'sheep shaggers', as people liked to call us, and for what happened the last time Aberdeen were there. With every bounce and sway the whole kettle got hotter. You felt that at any minute the whole thing could boil over, and sure enough it did!

Suddenly, all hell was breaking loose in their section on the opposite side of the ground. There was full-on fighting and a mob of Aberdeen was in the thick of it. Hundreds of fans started spilling on to the pitch to get out of the way of the melee. By now, the main body of the Aberdeen mob were going absolutely fucking mental, and there were lads trying to get over the fence and into the Motherwell fans next to us and threatening to invade the pitch from our end. It got too much for referee Andrew Waddell, who blew his whistle and quickly ushered the players and officials to the tunnel for safety. The fighting was now turning on the OB, who had been bolstered by reinforcements. Bottles, cans and coins were raining down as the riot continued, amid booing from the ordinary supporters for whom the game had been marred.

It took the initiative and bravery of Aberdeen's captain Willie Miller to bring things under control. Using the house PA system to address the crowd and appeal for calm, he then approached the trouble spot, as police separated the brawling mobs and encouraged Aberdeen fans to get back in their own section and settle down, otherwise the game would have to be abandoned! Only when there was a noticeable presence of stewards and police did the referee allow the players to come back out on to the pitch to continue the match. The play was delayed for what seemed like an age but in reality it was only somewhere between seven and ten minutes. The fighting, however, continued outside, as scores of supporters were ejected from the ground. The sound of sirens was clearly audible as the game was played out.

The tension in the ground had obviously had a bad knock-on effect on the players' performance and concentration, as six of them were booked, three from each side. It ended up a whitewash 4–0 result in Aberdeen's favour, with two goals from Strachan, and one each from Black and Hewitt completing a miserable day for Motherwell. As the lads sang 'so fuckin' easy!' and 'cheerio, cheerio, cheerio' to the early-departing Motherwell supporters, the sirens continued to peal out near the ground. Outside there were running battles and missiles being thrown as the massed police presence tried to ferry the Aberdeen mob away from the ground towards the station, leaving the folk who had travelled down on buses to worry about getting through the trouble zone without being attacked. This was always the downside to travelling on a coach if it had kicked right off. With the train, there was at least safety in numbers. On this occasion, we were fortunate enough to get through the hordes of traffic unscathed.

The following day, the papers reported that 14 Aberdeen lads had been arrested and charged with various offences. The battles with Motherwell continued, but it was not until 1985 that anything major happened.

AMBUSHED

Another meeting with Motherwell at Pittodrie has become legend in casual circles, and not only in Aberdeen. I can only tell you what I know and remember from that day. I got the train around lunchtime, with around 15 other trendies from Inverurie and Kintore. When we pulled into Dyce there were another ten or so lads on the platform, heading into the city for the day's action. There was a buzz on as one of the older lads told us of plans to ambush the Motherwell mob when they got off the train, somewhere on their route between the station and Pittodrie. When we got to Aberdeen there were more OB than normal in the station. The numbers were definitely more suited to a visit from the Old Firm. We usually did a bit of a tour of the station to suss out the nooks and crannies, to see if there were any strange faces loitering about.

On this day, we were ushered out of the side entrance, where the goods lorries and service vehicles used to gain access to the northbound platform. We went up the steps and crossed over to the Station Hotel, where half the lads headed in the direction of the Schooner bar and the rest headed for Union Street via Bridge Street. There were spotters and Under Fives dotted about near the bus station and the Schooner. We were told that there was a mob waiting in Crazy Daisy's bar to do the business. The bar was a split-level affair that had a wild reputation as it turned into a titty bar for the lunchtime punters, with go-go dancers on display. A bit like Sir Laffalot's, except of an evening, Crazy's was also a renowned gay haunt. So it was an ideal place to stage a pounce as nobody would be expecting it. Not from there!

I headed up to Union Street with three other lads to see what the word was in our bar in Belmont Street. Near the graveyard we ran into lads from Newtonhill and Portlethen that I had gone to school with. They told us that some of the nutters from Stonehaven were going to get on the Motherwell train and walk up to the ground behind them. We were also told that there was a huge mob of Under Fives, who were going to come at Motherwell side-on, and were a way up ahead at the top of Union Street. The buzz was immense! Lads were getting on buses down to the beach to sniff out the action, and everywhere I looked on the walk towards Pittodrie there seemed to be little clusters of lads, as was the usual sight when Rangers or Celtic came to town, or when there was a good visiting support expected.

The group I was in now numbered about ten, and, as we got to the Union Street end of King Street and headed straight down our usual route, we ran into some trendies who told us that they had heard it had gone off big time. We thought that by now the usual escort would be in place and that we would have to wait until after the match for some action. When we got to the ground there were stories flying around willy-nilly. Some people were saying that the ASC had all been nicked! We headed through towards the back of the South Terrace, while a load of other lads headed to the Beach End, as I think there was some work going on at the stadium around that time. We came across a huge bunch of lads, and again there were various versions of what had happened. One thing was clear: the OB were well informed and had been on hand in force to ambush the Aberdeen lads, just as they were about to do the same to the Motherwell mob. There was a gutted feeling among the lads, as the chatter turned to questions. So where the fuck was the Motherwell mob?

Just after the kick-off, I heard some more lads talking about what had happened at Crazy's. Apparently, Aberdeen had come out on to the road to go ahead with the Motherwell boys, and had easily had four times as many lads as the SS. As the ASC steamed towards them they were swamped by dozens of OB, who blocked off the road and nicked a whole bunch of lads. Worse still, it transpired that the SS had been escorted back to the train station and been seen off on a train for their own safety. In truth, I don't think many of them would have fancied it anyway, being housed in the Main Stand at twice the entry price of the Beach End. As sitting ducks, and with the climate of the day already obvious, they were put out of the city to avert a very nasty clash. In short, this meant that there was no chance of any action for a mob that was big enough to do the Old Firm! The day had been well and truly thwarted, with the OB being the only ones to get a result. The weekend's press reported that there had been 47 arrests.

DAN RIVERS

LOCOMOTION

I don't know how many people will remember the
Locomotion from back in 1985. I suppose that many will
say that the Locomotion was to do with a supposed
planned day out to Motherwell, at least according to the
press. Others will remember the Locomotion, as I do, as
the name we gave ourselves every away day in that season.

The Locomotion was about going on the train to
Rangers and Celtic, Hibs and Hearts, and having a
'rammy' everywhere we went. Which is exactly what we
did! By the time the 1985/86 season kicked off, there were
1,000-plus active Aberdeen Casuals, and we were taking
mobs of between 400 and 500 nutters to every decent
away game on the fixture list, with 700-plus lads turning
out to a home game against the Old Firm. I remember
when we played Celtic at home and needed just a draw to
win the league. It was a game of massive significance and
importance. I had been in one of our bars with some of
the regular loons and we got into Pittodrie a bit later than
usual for a fixture of this size. Because of this we had to
sit right down the front of the pack in the middle of the
South Terrace. Some lads were even doubled up on seats.
As the mob stood up and swayed a 'come on you Reds' in

the direction of the massed green-and-white support, I remember thinking to myself, There are easily a thousand boys in here today; just fucking look at this! That was a proud day to be an Aberdeen Casual, I can tell you!

With Aberdeen getting all the wrong media attention and because of what had previously gone off against Motherwell, there was no fucking way that anything was ever going to happen again, and certainly not by way of an Operation Locomotion assault on Motherwell. The media thought they had exposed a major operation – a military-style planned attack. I would like to think that the Aberdeen lads actually played the media on that one.

On 20 October 1985, one of the main Scottish papers ran a piece on the 'Sinister New Threat By Hooligans', as presented by their 'undercover man'. This guy had somehow apparently managed to get away with infiltrating every major casual mob in Scotland and had come up with the pearler that everyone 'hated and feared Aberdeen', and proceeded with various tit-bits of information regarding other mobs and their dress codes, exploits and so on. Also, in that particular paper, the undercover man wrote a piece entitled 'Casuals Plan New Riot' and this was supposed to be about an attempted 'action' at Motherwell that would be the 'Locomotion'. As with a lot of the journalism at the time, dates were inaccurate, as were the facts in many cases, but, hey, when did this ever matter to the tabloid press and their coverage of 'soccer casual exploits'? Another leading paper also did a piece with an 'undercover man' who had travelled to

Celtic with the Aberdeen mob, and his interpretation of the day's events was again predictably inaccurate.

As I've said, I would like to think that some of the lads played the media at their own game regarding the supposed planned riot. To my mind, there were three simple facts as to why there was never going to be another show with Motherwell, and had the media put the pieces together they would have seen it for themselves. Firstly, both Aberdeen Football Club and Motherwell Football Club were in no danger of ever letting another incident take place at Fir Park, and had allocated a very limited number of tickets to the Aberdeen support. There were certainly not enough to cover the supposed numbers that were 'exposed' in that article – a 'hardcore mob of 500 hooligans' – plus the regular Aberdeen away support.

Secondly, the police intelligence had become that tight at the football that there were double if not treble the amount of OB drafted in for games involving Aberdeen and the other clubs with an active casual element, and especially for this big operation. This would include mounted OB and dogs. There were indeed 'undercover operatives' trying to infiltrate many mobs and that was known to most of the top lads at various clubs, so everything became very tight-lipped and edgy in certain quarters of the scene. Nobody wanted to be jailed for doing the football. The sentences had become much heavier and the lads with form had started to get worried. For some, it was sadly too late.

Lastly, and by no means least, the supposed Operation

Locomotion was never going to happen because nobody really wanted to know about another visit to Motherwell, and certainly not on the grand scale that was reported. Granted, a few of the boys toyed with the idea of going down again 'just for the fun of it', and I believe that around about 100 or so did. The fact is that the point had already been well and truly made, and in truth it wasn't worth the effort or risk considering the recent events. It would have been just too bang on top and no fun at all to try to pull the same stunt a third time.

Besides, the scene in Scotland had developed and now there were far bigger fish to fry, with no disrespect intended towards Motherwell. Much bigger battles were going on, and not just with Celtic and Rangers either. Though both Old Firm teams had started to pull half-tidy mobs of 'dressed' lads together to try to take the fight to Aberdeen, and the clashes were getting a lot more manic, the real tasty battles of the day were going on against Hibs' Capital City Service. They had always put on a good show when Aberdeen came to town, but they had also turned trendy and almost doubled their numbers. This made them the biggest threat to Aberdeen's status, as Scotland's number one!

Chapter 4

MAYDAY

THE CASUALS

The Mayday bank holiday has always signified the start of the summer season, especially for those people involved in the hospitality, leisure and catering trades. For those businesses situated in the coastal regions, it is tourist time. Since as far back as the 1960s, it has also been the tradition of those in bike gangs and scooter clubs to descend upon the seaside and show themselves off. It is a chance for mods, scooterists, 1960s dressers and those adorned in the custom and club leathers of the bike gangs to gather and parade their customised Vespas and power bikes. Dressing up and heading to the beach for a pose and a pull has been the thing for many people, for many a year. It ranges from the teens to the city suits and groups of folk on a pissed day out looking for a laugh in the arcades and an ice cream.

In 1984, exactly 20 years from the whole mods and rockers scene in Brighton, it was clear to see that casual had well and truly taken over from mod. No more would the once 'modernist' dresser be accepted or tolerated in Aberdeen. Not on this day, Mayday, not on the street, and certainly not in the company of casuals. On this Mayday bank holiday I saw just how much the casual movement had taken over everything. Not content with taking over the terraces, casual had taken over the tradition and the style of the whole youth genre. Not only in Aberdeen, but also throughout the entire country!

On the day itself there were a few mods milling about, but only about 50 in total. Never was there any more than between ten and fifteen of them together at any given time, not to my certain knowledge anyway. By comparison, there were casuals dotted about everywhere, and at least a couple of hundred of them in total. I would say there were easily as many as there were down at Motherwell to take it to the SS in March. From Union Street to the Beach Boulevard there were dozens of clusters of lads wandering about. There was one especially distinctive group that was on the lookout for a bit of naughty business. These were the Under Fives. I recognised them from the football and they were up for picking off just about anyone. The reason I know this will become apparent later.

As the day wore on, I found myself heading down to the beach, where there were at least a hundred casuals playing football and milling about on the grass next to the Beach Boulevard. There were bikes buzzing up and down the Boulevard, which had a double lane going in each direction to allow for heavy traffic. The bikes were also on parade along the sea front. It was clear from the vibe among the lads at the beach that day that the substitute for a go with another team's mob was going to be a row with the 'smellies'. More and more bikes ripped up and down the road next to the growing mob of trendies, who started to launch missiles at the riders as they came by, with cheers going up every time they made a pass, just like a bullfight. And just like in a bullfight there was only ever going to be one outcome, and that was that the bull was going to get it severely!

At some time late in the afternoon the aggro proper was kicked off by a have-a-go trendy wearing glasses. This lad would turn out to be the gamest Red I would ever meet and my absolute favourite character in the Aberdeen mob! As one of the bikes made a pass, this lad ripped the top off a bin on the Boulevard and ran straight into the middle of the road and launched the lid at another on-coming biker. It was like the starter bell going off at the Grand National. All of a sudden all these lads in bright-coloured tops followed his lead. Suddenly there were bins getting smashed up everywhere and the contents were strewn about, as bottles, cans and indeed the bins themselves were readied for launching at the now-aware bikers. The attacks on the riders were followed up by loud cheers and shouts, just like at the football.

As the casuals started to get more and more wound up, feeding off the vibe of the events taking place, the attacks became more daring, with boys running into the road and trying to hit the bikers as they passed. One biker slowed down at one point, as if to make some sort of a challenge, and was swiftly swamped by a bunch of lads. He took a good dozen punches to the head and body, before burning off again. As he went round the roundabout and came back down the other side, clearly upset by the attack, he popped a wheelie and made for some lads who were in the road, as if jousting at them.

Similarly, a couple of other bikes ripped towards the casuals who were now standing in the road, queuing up to try to get a hit in. This went on for just over half an hour, when suddenly there was the crashing sound of a bike, followed by a huge roar. Some lads had dismantled a fence that had some chain on it and were swinging it in the road like a lasso towards an on-coming bike. I think it was the one that had been hit by the bin lid when it first went off. As the bike went down, a pile of lads steamed towards the fallen smelly and kicked him around a bit, before he scrambled back on to his bike and tried to break away. The OB, who had been cruising up and down also, were there in minutes. Most lads scattered in the direction of the amusements. Some went up town.

For some, though, this was just a taster. Up on Union Street and all over the city centre, mods and bikers alike were being attacked and chased all over the place, on and off their bikes and scooters. I was nearly on the end of it myself. Even though I had been doing the football and had been dressing trendy for a while, I got duped into having a 'take-the-piss, one-last-laugh' day out by some mates who had similarly turned trendy in the last year after being into the mod thing. Except that when I arrived in Aberdeen at 11.30am on a train from Insch, unable to return until 5.00pm because of the bank holiday timetable, little did I know that the last laugh would actually be on me. It had been agreed that we all had to wear something mod. So I turned up in a cycling top, Farahs and desert boots. Nobody else showed. Bastards!

After waiting two hours at the station, freezing fucking cold, I headed to the baker on Belmont Street and bought myself a couple of shepherds and beans and a soup to heat myself up. You know the rest of the story. I had seen one of the older casuals when I first arrived and he told me to watch myself. I did and I was lucky. Very lucky! As I sat in the ticket office at the train station, my head in my hands, thinking about what a nightmare the day had been, a tall red-headed lad opened the door and shouted at me, 'Where's all your mods now?' I just shook my head and said, 'I'm nae a mod, min.' Wise up! How could I have been such a dick? He just laughed and walked away. In the years to come, this same red-headed lad would be seen with ASC shaved into the back of his head and become a comrade at arms as we travelled all over the country with the Aberdeen mob. Twenty years and quite some history later, he was my first contact from those old and crazy days as I started to do research for the book, and he has been a solid friend ever since.

Over the years the whole casual movement has mushroomed into a massive, thriving scene worldwide. Back at home in the Granite City, the new blood and a few of the staunch old school are still in attendance now and then at the football, although in significantly smaller numbers than back in the 1980s. The row still continues over who is Scotland's number one. In my day, there was no doubt about it. It was Aberdeen. Fact! Since I've been away, though, all my old ASC mates have either got married or gone on to have families. Some have been marked and forced under ground. Some have just given up on the football altogether. Some lads, like me, went into the dance scene or moved away. A lot of lads have been jailed. Some are on their last warning. Other lads have been banned from attending football grounds or have bans stopping them from travelling out of town on match days. Other sentences, including fines and tags, have been dished out willy-nilly. For sure, the OB intelligence has put them in control of curbing any plans for a day out. Even with the internet and disposable mobile numbers, arranging a decent off has been stepped all over. As one of the chaps said recently, 'It's no fun any more.' Another said that he believed this season might see the end of the Aberdeen Soccer Casuals, saying, 'It's the end of an empire.' For all of us who have been involved, it's hard to believe that it could all be over!

Chapter 5

ABOUT HIBS

THE CASUALS

One of my very first visits to Easter Road was in January 1983. We had been drawn against Hibs in the third round of the Scottish Cup. I went down on a packed supporters' club bus from Dyce. There was a mixture of family supporters, beer monsters, a few older trendies and about five of us younger lads. We ended up in a convoy of about 15 coaches – some supporters' club buses and a load of football specials out of Guild Street bus station. We stopped halfway down for a toilet break and to freshen up, as you do when there are women and drinkers on the bus. We had already stopped for a 'motorway line-up', much to the amusement of passing motorists, as a load of lads were knocking back the

38

Tennent's! We joined up with lads on buses from Hazelhead and Ellon and decided that when we hit Edinburgh we would all meet up and go looking for some of our lads who were on a football special and the main service train, as arranged.

When we got to the bus station there were absolutely hundreds of Aberdeen supporters milling about. Most were going to have some sort of lunch before embarking on the walk to Easter Road. Some headed straight for the nearest bars. There were between 15 and 20 of us heading into this cafe just off Princes Street, with a load of other Aberdeen supporters in tow, when we heard this huge crash of glass going off about 200 yards away. This was it; it had gone off big time! Running up the road were about 100 local lads, all mixed in dress but mostly skins, and right behind them were 200 Aberdeen. On the approach to the ground, there was a running battle in progress, involving about 250 lads. I instantly recognised the Aberdeen boys by their dress. They were much trendier than the Hibs mob, who were still sporting the dress code favoured by punks and skins, like flight jackets, Harringtons and the odd leather. This little row must have gone on for a good five minutes, or what we saw did anyway. It had most likely been going on for some time before that. Knowing what I know now, I'm sure it had.

I didn't see any other incidents that day. Aberdeen won the game 4–1 and went on to retain the Scottish Cup in May against Celtic in the final at Hampden. This fixture against Hibs was my first time away from home

39

witnessing the more serious side of what the Aberdeen Soccer Casuals were about. This would be the year that I would start dressing the part – dressing like a casual. This would also be the year that I would have to grow up pretty damn quick if I wanted to be part of the Aberdeen mob and learn to fight. To fight like a casual: to 'steam in' and 'do the business', to watch out for the 'man on' your boys' back, and to 'stand your ground' when it went right off.

So how did I learn to fight? I was never one for scrapping, not in any way, shape or form. I was a 'back down and talk my way out of it' kind of lad. Although on the few occasions I had managed to get the bottle up to have a go, I did well enough. I suppose all I was missing was the confidence to just go for it. Not to be spiteful or a bully, but just to know that, if I had to fight, I would be good at it. I was given lessons in martial arts but they didn't count for anything when it really came down to it.

This real lesson would be driven home when I got my first proper battering as a casual – just for being a casual! Funnily enough, it was away from a football scenario, but the battering was because I was dressed like a 'poof', as the country lads put it. I lived outside Aberdeen and was surrounded by farmer types and local yokels, who all shopped at the same country stores. You know the type: 51 States jeans, big-tongued white trainers and rock T-shirts. I was at my first 'night out' at a hotel disco in a rural village north of Aberdeenshire. It must have been 1984 or 1985. It was *the* place to go for a night out in the sticks, and every underage bimbo with any show of titties was allowed in, along with all the country loons and the likely lads with a bit of peach fuzz on their top lip.

I had been drinking a few times at the Lodge Hotel near Insch, as they too had a 'relaxed' approach to the age of punters there, and my mate, also under 18, used to pinch his brother's motor for the night to get us there and back. This hotel disco, however, was supposed to be the business. So, at the behest of my cousin, a regular, who was even younger than me, I got dressed and went out with him for my first ever night out at a proper adult disco. He was done up poser-style: lemon pique shirt and grey sheen trousers with slip-on shoes. Gads. I was wearing bleached Levi's, Puma California and a pastel-yellow Lacoste polo, with a white button-over jacket to finish. The hair was in a flick with a bit of a step.

I remember drinking Woodpecker cider that got me drunk very easily and meeting mates of my cousin. Maybe four or five pints later, I was fucked. The end of the night came about, and as we spilled outside the fresh air got me and I blew chunks, big style. I think I might have got a slap for that off the bouncers at the hotel but not a bad one: just a whack up the side of the head and a quiet word to go home and sleep it off. There was a baker across the street from the place, and my cousin, who had pretty much left me to my own devices all night, was with some young dame in the mass of bodies outside it. I told him I was feeling rank and needed to get a taxi and get home, but he didn't seem too bothered by this, so I decided I would try to walk the two miles up the back road to where

I was staying. Why we do these things when we are steaming drunk and incapable of rational thought or action, I do not know, but I set to the task.

I got to a bend in the road and the lights of the village behind me were now a blur. A few cars passed me on my travels and all of a sudden there were a couple of lads walking towards me. Then the shit hit the fan. I was still in full spin-out mode and said hello to the lads. As I tried to walk between them, one of them clothes-lined me, and I was down with the kicks coming in thick and fast. One of them shouted at me, 'Who the fuck do you think you are, you casual bastard,' and the other screamed something like, 'You're a long way fae home, pal,' as they continued kicking me and keeping me down.

Then the car they had been in pulled up next to us and emptied, and the passengers started kicking me to fuck along with rest of them. It's amazing how quickly you sober yourself up when something very scary happens. I thank fuck in many ways that I was as trashed as I was on the Woodpecker I had necked in the hotel, or I would have been in a lot more pain. I kind of came to a bit and started kicking out. I took one of them down and scrambled through them to break away. I must have made a run for it because I ended up in a ditch, almost up to my knees in water and shit scared. One of them came in after me while the others came to the edge of the ditch, but he was still about ten feet from me.

They were all shouting shit at me about being a casual and how I was meant to be hard and that I was going to get battered to fuck and nobody would know. I tried to get over a barbed-wire fence at the back of the ditch and tore my jeans and leg and caught my jacket, but there was now some distance between them and me. I ran as fast as I could, paralytic drunk and kicked senseless, through a muddy field in the dark. After many falls I was now covered in mud from head to toe, but I must have disappeared from their sight. I heard them shouting, 'Where the fuck is he?' and one of them shouting something about killing me for getting him soaking wet.

I just ran and ran, until I went full pelt into another barbed-wire fence, tearing my jeans again. This time I grabbed hold of a plain wire behind it to steady myself and received a hefty jolt of electricity for my trouble. It was a cattle wire to keep the animals penned in. Undeterred and still fleeing for my safety, I made my way down the barbed-wire fence to a post and got myself up the fence, steadying myself as best I could, and hurled myself over it. I had gone roughly in the direction of a farm across from where I was staying, and eventually I made it across the main A96 and got home.

After a frantic complaint from my mother, the police came to the conclusion that I had managed to do this to myself and that I had imagined it all. I had kicked myself to fuck, fallen in the ditch and no local loons were involved. I had also managed to leave various hand and boot marks on my back and body that were still evident the next day, and the bruising and bumps were all down to me. This was, and still is, how it goes for outsiders or city folk trying to live out in the sticks. It was also a big fucking wake-up call that I needed to have my wits about me at all times and that I had to be able to handle myself from then on in, as there might be occasions when I would be outnumbered and need to show my mettle to stay alive.

I had managed to fight back and lash out at a cup replay against Celtic at Parkhead in 1984, and had been ready to fly in, had the need arisen, at other potential rows. But there hadn't been any other real occasions where that need had come about. There was Ibrox in November of that year, but I was there with a supporters' bus and not part of the go that went off outside the Broomloan Stand after the match that day. Not that the adrenalin wasn't kicking in anyway, as it always did when you visited these sorts of places. You had to be ready for anything in Glasgow – that was a fact. That night on that dark country road, I wasn't. That was the last day I ever went down without having a right good fucking go back.

After that there were occasions when there were foe coming ahead and I just went mad and ran into them screaming. I also went for it when I was outnumbered but sober enough to know that I could hurt at least one or two of them and maybe get a break or some back-up. This wasn't all just about casual warfare; it was the rules of street survival.

As I went to more and more games and got closer to the Aberdeen mob, I saw what was required of me and emulated my peers. I learned that the boys at my side were as passionate as I was about the team, the city and the mob's reputation, and that they were ready to fight for me, so I had to be ready to stand up for them and for myself. This gave me the confidence to handle violent situations a lot better than I once had. It didn't make me a hard man or an evil bastard, I just became streetwise and handy, and the rest is history.

But that day's observations at Hibs were the start of my candid education in the ways of the soccer casual in all its glory, an education that would serve me well. In the years to come there would be nothing quite like a day out at Easter Road for having a battle.

WASH-OUT

My first trip to Hibs on the train was a bit of a fucking disaster really. It was a shitty, miserable day for a start, which never did inspire a day out. Especially as nine times out of ten you would be dressed inappropriately. I was just wearing a shirt and jumper, instead of some sort of waterproof with a hood, which would have been more the business. To be fair, I was pretty much on edge, considering the way it had gone off on my previous visits to Easter Road and earlier battles at Parkhead and Ibrox that year. Like I say, though, this was my first trip with the boys to Hibs and there weren't a lot of lads that I knew in plain sight. I had got on the train with the mass of bodies and had intended looking about for my usual lot but ended up just taking a seat where I could. Not that I didn't believe in the lads' or my own capabilities. Aberdeen were Scotland's number-one mob and I was proud to be part of it! I had shown I was ready to do my part when necessary and that's all that mattered.

I remember standing between the carriages, talking to one of the older boys about the butterflies. He told me this story about how all the 'greats' got nervous before doing something big, and how even Elvis got nervous before every gig. 'And he was the King!' This guy likened every match to a gig. 'It just means you have respect for your work,' he said and burst out laughing. Then he said, 'Look, min, dinna take it so serious. This is the mentalest mob in the land.' I knew he was right, and just to finish things off on a funny he said, 'Just imagine one of these Hibee cunts givin' it to yer ma or your missus... it works for me.' Every time I saw him at a game after that, he would say 'your ma' or 'your missus', so that I kept my focus!

As I settled back among the throng of buzzing nutters, I started to set myself up for the battle that lay ahead. Some of the lads were talking about how 'you barely get off the train these days and the cunts are on ye'. The drizzle had turned to rain and I must have got lost somewhere, staring out of the window most of the way. Stones pinged off the windows at Dundee, as they would every away day by train, and then suddenly the atmosphere changed. Everybody just kind of sat up a bit and started to get a focused head on. You would look round at your crew for the day and give those all-knowing nods and acknowledgements. Some of the older lads were having a walk about the carriages and geeing the boys up, almost like a team talk. This was a definite feature of going away on the train with Aberdeen.

At the same time, though, there were also a few of the main faces going among the younger lads and telling them, 'If anybody runs, they'll get it back on the train.' How did the saying go? 'No kids, no runners, no scarves!' Yet nobody that got on a train with this mob could have any doubts about what it was that we were here to do or what was required of them. 'Stay tight, Aberdeen.' As Haymarket came and went, everybody was up and ready to go, doing up jackets and double-tying laces. Some lads were even removing their watches. All these mad little elements helped to build up the atmosphere on the train to absolute boiling point.

The top boys were already hanging out of the windows as we pulled into Waverley Station. The door handles were half-cocked, and then they were on the platform before the train had even come to a standstill. 'Come on, Aberdeen,' some of the lads shouted, banging tables and the roof as we left the train. Everybody was in a hurry now, jostling for position up the platform, trying to get nearer the front or seeking out the regular faces they were going to stand beside when it all went off. Some lads wanted to hit the rail bar to get some tins or a few wee bottles of spirits on the go. Most were following those in the know to the bars that Aberdeen liked to take over when they came to town. As we poured out on to Princes Street, it was clear that there was some fucking mob here.

DAN RIVERS

There were easily 250–300, plus the lads that were waiting at the rail bar for us to arrive. I can't remember the name of the bar that we piled into at the back of Princes Street. I just remember being grateful for the bottle of Beck's that got passed my way.

When we poured outside en masse, filling up the road with the expectant throng of buzzing nutters, I thought that Hibs had made an appearance, but, no, it was just time to head to the ground. I think we got about as far as Leith Street, when the mob just came to a standstill. There was no sign of any opposition anywhere, which was a complete anticlimax. After putting myself through hell with worry and overcoming it with the hunger for the fight, I was disillusioned when word filtered through from some locals that the game was off because of the weather. You could hear different boys saying 'wise up, min,' or 'min, ye've got te be joking' and plenty of 'I dinnae fuckin' believe this', as was my own comment at the time. Everybody was fuming. What a fucking waste of time. Shit weather, no game, a wasted train ticket and, most importantly, where the fuck were Hibs?

We looked for them on our walk back but there was nobody in sight to even take it out on. The OB picked up on us as we got down towards Princes Street again and saw us right into the station. There were a fair few of them in there and a Black Maria or two on standby. They knew that we were fizzing and just wanted us out of the city without incident. Most of us resigned ourselves to the fact that it was just a dud day all round.

But suddenly there was a rush of bodies and a shout of 'come on, Aberdeen' went up. As the roar echoed in the station and we tried to break out quick, the OB moved in and blocked our path. Some Hibs had shown and given it the large and then bolted. We were choking to get out and at them. Some of the lads made it up the steps, while others made attempts to get out up the ramp. Those lads that broke through would have to do it for the rest of us, who were told in no uncertain terms that we would be nicked if we didn't fuck off back to Aberdeen on the first northbound train. They waited about and obligingly saw a load of us off. What a fucking wash-out the day had been!

But my next visit to Easter Road would be very different indeed.

99 BIG SOCCER REDS

That next trip was in March of 1985. There were no such butterflies this time. After the sad fucking effort on the last day out here, rain or no rain, this time we didn't give a fuck. There was a huge mob on the main service train and a fair few had already gone ahead on an earlier football special. I had a lot of lads that I knew around me, including some of the Inverurie boys and some of the regulars that were getting used to seeing my face. The all-round confidence on the train was very high. Our team was on the verge of having the league away again. A couple more good wins and we would be set up for a winner-takes-all home clash with title challengers Celtic. If we stuffed them, the league would surely be ours. Well, that was the plan anyway, and we were looking forward to having hundreds of Tims about in our own manor to reciprocate their usual warm and friendly hospitality at Celtic Park!

Meanwhile, back at Easter Road, things were not looking too clever for Hibernian Football Club. A few more defeats and they were in the relegation zone. If that wasn't enough to set the flames blazing under the already boiling cauldron of hate, then nothing would be! The train journey passed by so quickly it was scary. I remember some of the lads talking about Dundee and whether they were going to bother next month and how mental Ibrox had been in November. When the subject of Hibs came about again I must have switched off. Tunnel vision. When the train tannoy announced, 'We are now approaching Haymarket. Haymarket Station,' it was just like some mad flashback – a deja vu. Here we were again. Time to shape up and ship out. Everyone was champing at the bit now. We were tightened up and tidied up, and ready to rock and roll!

I was up and heading into the crush for the doors joining the two carriages behind where I'd been sitting when we rolled into Edinburgh Waverley once again. The shouts and chants of positive affirmations among the lads once again rang out around me. 'Let's do this, Reds' and 'come on then, boys' and 'we're nae leavin' here the day without a fucking result!' A lot of boys had it in the back of their heads what a fuck-up the last visit there had been. I don't remember any such niceties as stopping for a drink or anything else. On this day, the battle was all, and what a fucking battle it was!

I remember the mob, totally solid, filling the road ahead and far behind, and the crazy buzz of the boys. There were lads fanning out and running up steps and standing on car bumpers, trying to see ahead for any sign of the Hibs mob. As we approached the turn-off from Leith Street into Leith Walk and filled London Road, the whole mob broke into a canter. And just as we were approaching Easter Road it went off. The first battery of missiles flew through the air towards us, including bottles, bits of tarmac and building brick, stones and coins, bits of roadwork equipment and other masonry.

It was here that I got my first look at the Hibs mob. They looked to have about the same numbers as us, maybe 300 or so, making their way towards us halfway up the road. The Hibs started chanting at us and menaced about in the middle of the road. We stood back as the lads at the front gave the hand signs to 'come ahead'. As they drew closer the shout went up to 'stand, Aberdeen, stand'. This was echoed by our foe as a very tense moment went down: the two mobs sizing each other up. There was a play to make a bit of a charge at us from the front of the Hibs mob, and suddenly the shout went up. 'Come on then, Aberdeen, let's do it,' and we moved on them like a swarm! There was pride and reputation at stake here, and everybody wanted a piece of it.

To be fair, only the front 100 or so lads got a hit on target as the Hibs mob backed off. As they splintered, the whole middle section of Aberdeen, which I was a part of, steamed after the little breakaway groups, but the whole idea was to stay tight and stick together – to do the job as one, which we pretty much did. Hibs themselves then gathered, and the boys at the back of their mob pushed forward and launched yet more missiles as they charged us, their front-runners picking up debris from the first wave of attacks, like a cone and various other missiles and bottles, and throwing them into our path once again.

Aberdeen moved into the middle of the road to meet them, and once more shouts went up, the roar of the lads filling the air as we charged them again. This time the fighting was fierce, as loads stood and fought. It was just the most mental buzz you could imagine. Punches and kicks flew in from everywhere as we steamed in! Once again, though, there were only between 100 and 150 lads who actually got stuck in, as the Hibs mob backed off again and the battle went into yet another time-out as the mobs regrouped. Some of the Hibs made to come back at us but backed right away as we went to engage them again. This time, though, the familiar sounds of the sirens that signalled the arrival of the OB could be heard. The police soon filled the middle of the road, lifting lads from both mobs, sending Hibs on their way and herding the rest of us up for an escort. We knew then that it was all over.

More sirens were audible as we approached the narrow

bridge leading up to the ground still under heavy supervision. We were taunted by some of their strays but the job had already been done. Aberdeen weren't interested in battling strays and nobody else wanted to get nicked. Inside the ground the lads were jubilant. We had definitely fared better than Hibs and backed them off on Easter Road. We joined the rest of the travelling Aberdeen support in a loud chorus of 'Aberdeen, Aberdeen, Aberdeen'. We were in carnival spirits as our team romped in the goals: 1–0, 2–0, 3–0! The Hibs support booed their own team and us, and coins and missiles were thrown at the referee and the players. The game ended 5–0 to Aberdeen, with Eric Black getting a hat-trick and the match ball. The Hibs support threw yet more missiles on to the pitch as they booed their sinking team off the pitch.

I can't remember anything after the game. The OB were with us in the ground and there was a heavy escort to the station for the train home. Only after reading the Sunday papers did I see the news. During the running battles on Easter Road, one of the Hibs casuals had slipped on the debris and got 'bounced on'. Apparently he was in a really bad way. A week later and everybody knew the words to the song that went to the melody of the number one Nena track '99 Red Balloons'. As the Aberdeen mob gathered in their seats that week, another league title beckoning, the song rang out as it had so many times on the house PA system at Pittodrie. But this time the words were different. It went '99 Big Soccer Reds, Bouncing On * * *'. I'll let you fill in the blanks for yourselves.

DAN RIVERS

A TALE FROM ONE OF THE LADS – THE PETROL BOMB INCIDENT

I can remember the word spreading round the terraces that Hibs were going to be waiting for us after the game. No surprise there, I thought, as most away days to Edinburgh provided us with more than enough challenges to Aberdeen's title. Ever since I had started going to the football on a regular basis, Hibs had been my favourite fixture. Something about it had always appealed to me. The crowds, the danger, the buzz and, best of all, the bridge. Anything could happen at a Hibs match. They always provided a challenge and we were always more than up for accepting it. My first memories of football violence were of fighting at Hibs away. No casuals in that day, just loads of skinheads but up for it all the same.

All the way down on the train we had been told that this was the big one and we weren't far wrong. Hibs were definitely after Aberdeen's title as the undisputed champions of Scottish football and the motley crew of rogues, fighters and trendies that sat on this train were all that stood in their way. I wasn't worried. I knew that the ASC had more than enough numbers to take anything that Edinburgh could muster – and more.

For more than five years we had been travelling across Scotland leaving chaos and newspaper headlines in our wake and today was to be another chapter in our (as yet) brief history. The usual faces were all there and like most Saturdays away they all were quite happy to while away the journey by playing cards and taking some mug's money off them. Everyone knew the score. No runners. No shitters. We would stand and take what Hibs could throw at us before returning the favour.

We spilled off the train and made our way towards the ground, a mass of pastel colours, trendy trainers and smart haircuts. We knew that no one liked us, but, as Millwall so famously sang before Rangers ICF appropriated it, we didn't care. The police were waiting for us as we exited the station and some lads began splitting off from the main group eager to find some action on their own. That was the thing about Aberdeen, even though we were at our best as a team, we also worked very well individually. On many an occasion I had seen a lone ASC member wade into a mob of opposing fans and scatter them. That was what separated us from so many pretenders to our throne. We had the faces and the bravado to turn the tide in our favour. I often wondered what our rivals thought when one or two of our number would wade into them fists flailing and feet flying.

The game itself was instantly forgettable – to me at least. I mostly ignored the game and laughed, joked and scoured the opposite terraces for potential targets. Hibs were the dominant force in Edinburgh and it was to their credit that they had turned out in numbers today for our arrival. They were watching us as we watched them. There didn't seem to be that much of them but I didn't let that fool me. I knew the CCS often missed the game so they could wait in bars nearer the city centre and knew that a welcome committee would be waiting for us on our walk back to the station. I could only see a few CCS standing on the terraces watching us and weighing up our numbers just as I was doing to them.

At the final whistle we streamed out into the waiting streets, hearts pumping and eyes staring. The time had come. My eyes were on the bridge as we made our way towards London Road. I loathed that bridge and for good reason. As a 16-year-old I had crossed it into a line of skinheads and instantly froze before the cheer went up from behind me and legions of older ASC steamed through and scattered the boneheads back to their Leith hovels. I was older and wiser and knew that Hibs would not be waiting so close this time. Instead they would wait on the side streets off of Easter Road and make their attacks from there. Calls went up from the main lads for everyone to stand when the trouble started and soon after the air was alive with shouts of approval from everyone.

Sure enough, once on London Road the fun began. Shouts were going up from every direction and I saw groups of ASC break ranks and run towards their CCS rivals. Police were running up the road in an attempt to stop the fighting but sheer force of numbers prevented them from stopping the scuffling. The street was a mass of whirling bodies. Hibs were attacking from all sides and the thin blue line was being stretched even thinner. I ran and launched myself into the first Hibee that came within range. The rule of fighting for me was make sure you hit the other person first and hardest to dissuade them from making a comeback. If they know you can pack a wallop and are game, then they'll think twice about retaliating. His face and bravery crumbled as I hit him and he turned to look for back-up. Hibs at this point were all over the place and the police on duty did not know where to start. My opponent melted away into the crowd as I saw people being dragged away by the scruff of their necks and thrown against walls, so I did likewise. The police down here were bastards when they nicked you and I had no intentions of becoming another Saturday afternoon statistic, held in a cell all weekend.

Eventually, order was restored somehow and the scattered groups of ASC pulled together. We moved along slowly with scores of police between the CCS and us, each member staring across the road at his counterpart silently wishing that the police would just leave us to it. I could never understand why the police just couldn't give us, say, ten minutes alone to sort things out. Occasionally we got lucky and this would happen but as the years passed and the police grew wiser to our tactics then the opportunities became less and less.

Once I turned the corner on to London Road and saw the numbers that were gathered for this confrontation, I realised that today was one of the best turnouts there had been for a long time down in Edinburgh. Through the bushes at the side of the road I could see smaller groups of CCS waiting and watching. This was a favourite tactic of theirs, obviously picked up from watching old Vietnam war movies and used to great advantage against lesser teams. However, Aberdeen, after years of travelling to Easter Road, were more than capable of dealing with this urban form of guerrilla warfare. Probably because of the sheer numbers, they kept their distance from us and eventually melted into the side streets hoping to ambush us near the station.

We continued walking and near the end of the road we saw our chance and about 15–20 of us cut off and kept walking towards Princes Street where we thought we would have the best chance of finding more CCS. We stuck together, each of us knowing how dangerous our task was and in no doubt what would be required of us if and when we found our foes. The group consisted of a few older ASC, some around my own age and a small amount of Under Fives.

This didn't worry me as I knew our Under Fives were amongst the most vicious in the country, as another Hibs casual had found out to his cost earlier in the year. Down he went and about a hundred pairs of Adidas Gazelles relentlessly kicked him in the head as they ran past without the slightest thought about the consequences. It was a sad day in ASC history but at least the poor guy recovered from his life-threatening injuries. The moral of the story from that day onwards has been if you go down in front of the Aberdeen mob then don't expect to get up too easily afterwards.

At one point I managed to move ahead of the police escort and join in with a smaller band of ASC that had moved further up the street. Police escorts were not the exact science that they are now, where you are practically hemmed in on all sides by police, vans, horses and dogs. Back then you had a thin blue line stretched to breaking point simply by the size of the mobs involved. It was no exaggeration to say that, for some away games, the ASC numbered 500 and sometimes more, depending on the opposition and the importance of the game. Cup ties were always guaranteed to bring out the big guns though. The faces, for one reason or another, had stopped going regularly and instead only attended cup games. There were some of those faces in attendance today and one had managed to attach himself to this group, which I, for obvious reasons, was quite glad of.

We moved through the crowded streets of Saturday shoppers like a pack of wolves on the hunt. To the shoppers we were nothing special, a bunch of young men walking through the streets. We were deliberately quiet so as to avoid being detected by any police and to avoid scaring away our targets. We knew they were here; all we had to do was find them. We knew what to look for. Hibs dressed just like us. They were our equals, fashion-wise, which made them easy to recognise. Most towns we visited, the opposition were dressed like tramps, with only a few notable exceptions such as the likes of Motherwell and Rangers. At least those boys made an effort, not like some of the jokers who stood on the terraces of Dundee or Parkhead. They were an embarrassment not only to themselves but also to the Scottish scene as a whole. At one point someone spotted a couple of likely lads standing in a doorway ahead and motioned for us to move in but as the front two boys closed in on them they were seen and the two lads ran off into the crowds. Just as well for them, I thought. At least we now knew there were some Hibs about and the sighting of those two renewed our hopes of finding some action. Suddenly a roar went up and through the crowds came the sight we had been waiting for. A group of CCS came charging towards us from further up the road, screaming and shouting in an attempt to send panic through the ranks.

'Hi-bees... Hi-bees... Hi-bees!'

All who met and fought them knew their familiar battle call. This call simply made us bond together as one and attack en masse. We were Aberdeen and it took more than shouting to scare us. We spread out and flooded across the road as we ran towards them. The traffic stopped and for one split second I thought that we could perhaps do with more numbers as Hibs had a good number of boys intent on fighting us. That thought however was halted by the sudden appearance of a flame in the sky, like a flaming portent of doom. There are certain things in your life that you can never forget, first pets, marriages, deaths and the birth of your first-born. To that list I would like to add something else: the sight of a petrol bomb flying through the air towards you!

I stopped running and watched as it made its journey through the air before finally coming to a sudden explosive halt on the main road not ten feet in front of me. The road instantly burst into flames and for an instant all was quiet. The people in the cars looked as stunned as we were. We were all shocked and no one knew quite what to do. It was so unreal. We had come here to fight Hibs not be petrol-bombed on their main street! Both mobs backed off, aware that this new development was not one that we were used to. Even the police who had suddenly appeared from nowhere looked shocked at the sight of Princes Street in flames.

The sight of the police was more than enough encouragement for us to make our retreat so we turned and started running back towards the station. Small groups of CCS followed us, obviously encouraged by the sight of the ASC on their toes thinking that we had been scared by their mob's appearance. How wrong they were. Hand-to-hand fighting was our speciality and Aberdeen feared no one. What we very perceptibly did fear were petrol bombs being launched and exploding in front of us.

Our retreat to the station was a free for all. We all split up and made for where we knew the main group of ASC would be standing in Waverley Station. Three of us ran though the Princes Mall to the amazement of the shoppers there. They probably thought we were shoplifters or something due to the speed we were moving through the crowds. The small group of CCS that had been chasing us soon stopped as we neared the entrance to the station. Some had beaten us back already and fellow ASC eager to find out exactly what had just happened soon crowded round. Tempers flared and there was talk of returning to Princes Street to find the CCS responsible but in the end the amount of police that flooded into the station prevented any chance of a rematch on the streets of Edinburgh.

We eventually boarded our train and all talk was on the day out. The fighting afterwards, whether Hibs had Oldham with them, the amount of police and, most importantly of all, the petrol-bomb incident. People gathered round tables to hear first-hand accounts of what had happened and swore revenge on the CCS on their next visit to Pittodrie. Whether they would show at all was a good point as most mobs in Scotland did not seem to know their way to Pittodrie, as was apparent by their no-shows, year in, year out. I wasn't really surprised as a trip to Aberdeen must have been a daunting task, to say the least, particularly when you took into account the walk from the train station to the stadium. The bigot brothers army of scarfers would often do it in the early to mid-1980s but this was becoming more and more of a rarity, as the walk would involve them running the gauntlet of hundreds of ASC eager to confront them on their journey to Pittodrie.

I noticed that our train was slowly grinding to a halt just beyond Haymarket station and the reasons behind this soon became clear as dozens of police flooded on to the train. Not only police but also sniffer dogs were boarding the train for a reason which soon became apparent as they started urging the dogs to inspect our shoes and us. I suddenly realised that I could be picked up for no other reason than simply being in front of the petrol bomb itself and I hoped that the dogs' sense of smell wasn't as good as the police were expecting!

Voices became raised as one ASC member started berating the police, asking them if they actually thought we had travelled all the way down to Edinburgh from Aberdeen with a petrol bomb in our pockets, went to the game, walked back into the city centre and then thrown it at ourselves. Ripples of laughter ran through the carriage at this outburst. I could see even the officers on the train realised the stupidity of their actions but no doubt the order had come down from above and had to be acted on. I can just imagine the Chief Constable sitting in his office fuming about those 'bloody casuals' from Aberdeen coming to his city and throwing their petrol bombs on Princes Street! He must have shat it when that first report came in over his radio!

Eventually the police left the train, but not before taking a few statements and sniffing a few jumpers, leaving us to continue our journey home in relative peace. I can laugh about that day now, but back then that had been one of the scariest things I had ever seen at the football. Hibs had been mental at the best of times and I had seen many an ASC head home covered in blood but at least they had been able to go home. Had that bomb landed closer to some of us there then it would have caused a major injury or even death.

That wasn't what football violence was about to me and I'm sure the vast majority of the lads that enjoyed a tear-up at the football thought the same. It wasn't enough to

DAN RIVERS

put me off going again but I would be very wary of any more trips to Easter Road in the future. Thanks to LvC for his contribution.

Chapter 6

ABOUT 1985

THE CASUALS

In footballing terms, 1985 was yet another excellent year in the history of Aberdeen Football Club. This had started off in January with another top-class performance at Pittodrie against the Old Firm enemy of Rangers. A sound 5–1 thrashing was bestowed upon the visitors that day, providing proof, if indeed there was any more proof required to convince everybody, that Aberdeen FC were no longer intimidated by the likes of Rangers and Celtic. It was fair to say that Aberdeen had become the new dominant force in Scottish football. This form would continue throughout a season in which they would retain their crown as the Premier League champions with a draw at home to the other half of the Old Firm, Celtic.

That game was a special day indeed for many reasons. One of the main factors was that it was our captain and team motivator, Willie Miller, who scored the all-important headed equaliser after the Tims had stolen the lead with a predictable penalty. I remember him spinning back on himself, almost losing his balance, as he nodded the ball into the back of the net. The look of sheer delight and relief on his face was there for all to share as he ran right up the pitch alongside us in the South Terrace, waving a defiant and triumphant fist. I remember the whole Aberdeen support in the ground going daft and singing out 'championis, championis, all the way, all the way, all the way' in jubilation, followed by repeated choruses of 'one Willie Miller, there's only one Willie Miller'. And, right enough, in all the years that I was in Scotland, there was never a player quite like him. Our dominance on the park that year was completed by a 3–0 League Cup final victory over Hibs at Hampden Park.

Now, as I have stated already, my buzz came from being part of Aberdeen's mob, being right in the thick of it all. Wearing the right clothes and having the right attitude were all part and parcel of it. The battles and being prepared to stand and fight were also part of it. The fight was against the opposite number in the other team's mob, not innocent supporters and not members of the public. There were just these unspoken rules and everybody was meant to adhere to them. Nobody I knew wanted to kill anyone. Nobody I knew ever carried or used a blade in battle. Aberdeen had never needed to use blades to get a reputation. Other weapons were only ever used in the heat of the fight: like throwing bits of rubble back at the other mob if they had chucked them at us in the first place. I won't deny that this did take place from time to time, as was necessary, but nobody I knew went out to a game tooled up. Ever.

But in 1985 the whole casual scene was starting to change. The Scottish media had weekly, sometimes daily, stories involving casuals rolling hot off the press. The Hibs Capital City Service had emerged as a new force to be reckoned with and the Aberdeen Soccer Casuals were on everybody's shit list at every level, everywhere. Every mob in Scotland hated them and had been on the receiving end of it, whenever the rival mobs had clashed. South of the border, West Ham's ICF (Inter City Firm) were getting the same media attention as Aberdeen, and hooliganism involving English teams was at an all-time high, or low depending on how you look at it, with dozens of deaths in football-related incidents across the country and abroad.

There was the death of a young fan after a wall collapsed as Leeds and Birmingham fans ran riot. There was a fire at Bradford that killed 56 fans. Then there was the death of 39 fans in the Heysel Stadium in Belgium, as Liverpool and Juventus fans clashed on the terraces in a horrific live televised European Cup final game. Also in 1985, there was a full-scale pitched riot between Millwall and Luton supporters in an FA Cup clash, where hundreds of fans tore the stadium apart and battled with the police.

Meanwhile, back in Scotland, Aberdeen were at the centre of some of the most publicised incidents involving confrontations with other groups of rival casuals, including the 'Ambush Of Away Supporters' and 'Casuals Plan New Riot' headlines I've already mentioned. Then there was the 'Near Death' of a Hibs casual, who had been critically injured, after a clash on Easter Road and the 'Petrol Bomb' incident, when Aberdeen returned later that year.

There had also been some of the biggest scenes of anarchy in and around Ibrox in many a year after Aberdeen's humiliation of Rangers in their own back yard led to a mass exodus of Rangers fans from the ground in an attempt to get at the away support that almost ended in a riot. Among the headlines were 'Fury As Fans Storm Ibrox Pitch' and '48 Held After Ibrox Battle'. There had also been numerous incidents at grounds across Scotland that had made the local news, including numerous clashes in Dundee at a game in March.

The media were having a feeding frenzy, as so-called undercover reporters and police worked together to try to undermine the growing casual scene. New tougher measures were put into place and policing and security was tightened as the powers that be set about stamping on the phenomenon. The official Glasgow Celtic fanzine, *The Celtic View*, described casuals as the 'new cancer' in Scottish football and reported that the 'disease' had reached 'epidemic proportions' in Aberdeen!

Chapter 7

GETTING DRESSED

THE CASUALS

As I have mentioned already, the clothes and getting dressed were as much a part of the movement as the violence that was associated with the casuals themselves. It would be nigh on impossible to pinpoint the exact dates of the many changeovers of labels and styles, as, you boys in the scene will know, things used to move on so quickly. One minute you were up front, a trendy, and the next you were out of fashion! It was that quick. I will however do my best to pay homage to some of the items that attributed so much to the look that was unique to the casual back then. The look was different; it was sharp and a cut above anything else that was happening on the streets in Aberdeen and, indeed, anywhere else in Scotland and for the most part in Britain as a whole!

When I first started to take notice of them, during that 1982/83 season, there was a mixture of labels on display. Pringle lambswool jumpers were a definite part of the uniform, although by the time I had started dressing the diamond pattern had been and gone, which is a real shame because I loved the look of some of those. I did, however, get in on the block-pattern Pringles and also had a few plain-coloured ones too. Some lads also wore Pringle and Pierre Cardin roll-necks, often in combination with a V-neck jumper. Lyle and Scott had some very smart-looking jumpers around at that time too. I even seem to remember seeing a yellow Slazenger V-neck on one of the older lads back then. Polo shirts were also in evidence among the boys, with Lacoste being a favourite. These came in the same sort of bright pastel colours as the Pringles, with lemon and pink being the favoured colours. People wore Kappa and Ellesse, and some of the older lads had labels like Sergio Tacchini and Fila and more dressy labels like Armani and Dior.

A lot of the lads sported Farah trousers, while faded Lois jeans and Lois cords were also popular. Most had a split or mud-flap in them. I remember brown, burgundy and plum Lois cords, not forgetting the jumbo cord look, which was big for a while, and cords from Wrangler and Lee. Then there were Levi's bleached jeans, which if I remember rightly came in with a 14"–15" bottom, as did the Lee jeans. Flares came in and out of fashion, with most sitting around the 18" mark, frayed or unfrayed, always with a good length. It was all about the way your jeans or cords sat over your trainers or shoes.

In the shoe department there was all sorts going on. I got into it just in time to catch the mad wedge trainer thing. I had Puma wedges, the first pair being white leather with silver or gold trim. Then there was a navy suede Puma wedge with pale blue trim, the California. Some wore Adidas Trimm-Trab, others Diadora Borg Elite. I went through Puma Dallas and G Vilas at school but also got into Adidas. There were Nike and Reebok running shoes that went up through the price range. The one-upmanship was all part of it, with some lads going for the dearest pair on the block, just because they could. Although I seem to remember at one point that most of the Aberdeen mob were wearing Adidas Samba, which were pretty much accessible to every pocket. I had a few pairs of those and also went through a Gazelle phase.

Apart from trainers there were plenty of other options. There were Hush Puppy shoes, desert boots and brogues. Clarks also had some very comfortable and trendy-looking shoes, particularly the Polyveldts and Wallabees. There were Kickers boots and shoes and Pod shoes and sandals did the rounds for a wee bit too. Next had a very nice range also, including the boat shoe, moccasin boots and shoes and the deck shoe. And I have to mention Timberland boots and moccasins, which were worn by a good portion of the lads at some time or another and of course the Gucci loafers!

On the jacket front, cagoules were popular when I first turned trendy, with Adidas and Kappa being the favourites. Barbour wax jackets were about for a bit, early- to mid-80s, but in winter a lot of the guys went for ski jackets, with Berghaus bubbles and Ellesse being popular among the lads with plenty of lolly! Otherwise out in the sticks people wore Campri jackets and the odd Nevica. Again, it was down to the moment as the look just kept changing. In 1984 there was a bit more mix and match about the casual look, and, although lads were still wearing designer gear, the label thing wasn't as 'show and tell' as it had previously been. Saying that, the older lads in our mob, the founder members, were still full-on dressers and the younger lads were frowned upon for being scruffs.

The hairstyles changed along with the look, and wedges and flicks gave way to either shorter hair, maybe slicked or spiked, or the total opposite – the shaggy look, with longer on the top. Somewhere in there was the famous back perm and that footballer look – you know the one! I personally started with a flick, then had it short and spiked, then mopped and curly on top, came out of the 1980s with a middle-swept Dougal job, before finally, dare I say it, a ponytail!

As we moved into the mid-1980s I was wearing Ball jeans and Classic Nouveau, Ciao and Pop 84. I remember this clothes shop on Belmont Street that had all the labels and all the top items that were the choice of the trendies at the time. I got this Ciao T-shirt from there with a rose on it – it was a beautiful garment and it has stuck with me to this day. Other Aberdeen clothes shops that spring to mind from that time include the shop at the top of Union Street that did Jaeger and the boutique up near Golden Square. Pringle could be bought at Arnotts and the golf shops. Then there were these hooded jackets that everybody had in all sorts of colours. I had a bright-yellow one. These were worn either with the hood in the collar and zipped up, or usually with the hood out, jacket half or fully open and off the shoulder a bit. This look was as important as the jeans over the trainers and the haircut. We got escorted out of Ibrox in 1985 and *The Sunday Post* did a feature with a photo of us (I can't remember if it was the front page or not), but nearly every lad in the photo had that look. Jacket off the shoulder, flicked fringes, hands in pockets, with baggy, flared or mud-flapped jeans over the trainers. It was the casual look.

It was around this time that lapel pin badges made an appearance. With so many teams having mobs of trendies turning out on a Saturday, it might be said that it was difficult to tell the mobs apart. I believe that we knew our own lads and in fact knew lads from every other mob in Scotland, just as they knew us. All the same, pin badges were seen on shirt lapels and jumper collars of lads all over the country. The one that was favoured among the lads that wore them in our mob was available from Roselyn Sports on Hatter Street in Aberdeen for a pound.

When I take a look around at the clothes that the youth are wearing now, it's like the whole fashion thing has gone full circle and gone back to the look that we, the casuals, pioneered. It's like stepping back in time. Flared jeans and cords, some with a split or mud-flap, and quality trainers, mainly the classics that we would hunt out so as to be up-front. Then there's Burberry. Especially Burberry. Every bird on the block has got a bag or scarf these days, be it snide or not. And there are those dreadful look-alike rip-offs. Shit quality material with mismatched lines in minging colours. You see kids as young as ten wearing the Burberry check now. Back in the day it was only worn by city gents, scone shop housewives and the hooligan element known as the casuals! I still have my original golf jacket and the removable collar tab is still in place. My dark beige lambswool Burberry scarf, also 20 years old, was pinched at a friend's funeral, last Halloween. Ah, the levity of the petty minded. I just hope that the thief will enjoy it for another 20 years and give it the same love I did.

My own personal favourite has always been Aquascutum: the gentleman's check and the hooligan's choice. The two main checks were very big within the Aberdeen mob. As the fashion train kept rolling and we moved into the last third of the decade, more labels came in and out but the all-out look became far easier to achieve without having to be decked out head to foot in top-of-the-range designer gear. No matter what, though, the boys always had quality footwear and at least one label on display, and obviously the lads with the money and the senior members of the Aberdeen mob always dressed to the nines. Labels like Chipie, Chevignon, Ton-

Sur-Ton, C17 and Naf Naf were joined by the likes of Marc O'Polo, Hugo Boss, French Connection and Ralph Lauren on the backs of the Aberdeen mob. Stone Island also made its first appearance around this time.

It was around this time that the whole casual thing slowed right down. The fashion labels within the look stayed pretty much the same for a while and the numbers attending the football dropped off. Clubbing and drugs played a massive part in the setback within casual culture at the time. Also police intelligence had increased ten-fold and sentencing was getting more severe. When I left Aberdeen there was still a good-sized mob in attendance at most decent games and the wearing of quality-name labels was still prevalent.

It would be impossible to name all the items that were in at one time or another. But I will do my best to give you some of the more important items in the scene during the time that I haven't mentioned already! There was the Fila Bj Bjorn Borg jacket, the Fila Bj velour tracksuit top and the Fila tracksuit with pop-off buttons on the sleeves and bottoms. There were Tacchini tracksuit tops and polo shirts, Armani jumpers, Principles striped tops and Benetton rugby shirts. The Pop 84 baseball jacket with the patches was a bit special. Leather puffa jackets also made an appearance. Tweed suit jackets, Pepe jeans and the tag/keyring thing that went with wearing those jeans. There was also a thing with lads wearing beads in their laces and, of course, the multiple Kickers poppy tags. Naval Artic jackets and Best Company jackets and jeans,

Hugo Boss sweatshirts, paisley shirts, short-sleeved check shirts, Sonnetti jeans, St Michael Knitwear, Burlington argyle socks, Converse baseball boots, Lacoste golf jackets, golf umbrellas, Head holdalls, Peter Storm jackets, and not forgetting the John Menzies hat! The list is really endless, but you Aberdeen lads in the know will remember them all!

Chapter 8

DAYS AWAY WITH THE JUTES

THE CASUALS

When I first sat down to decipher my scrambled notes and started writing I was going to call this chapter 'Dundee Toilet Crew', simply because that was the lasting memory, the stink of piss, and that prompts my memory of Dundee (well, to be more precise, Dens Park). Nasty but true! Thinking about it now I get a thick clag in the back of my throat. Gads. Every time I went there the fucking troughs were blocked, so you were actually stood in other people's piss when you took a leak. In your best quality trainers or shoes too!

Strangely, not a lot springs to mind about Tannadice. The United were a bogy team back then and had a bit of pride about their ground and their team, and they were financially better off than their derby rivals across the city. But while we had a lot of good days out there and the Utility is a combined mob, strange though that may be, it is games against Dundee that I remember us having a bit of a dance at the most. I might have taken the piss, quite literally, at the start of this chapter, but it is only right to point out that a fair few of the Dundee boys were quite game and, although a lot of our lads didn't rate it as a real day out, a visit to Dundee would always yield some sort of sport!

I remember one of the first times I went to Dundee, not only was I completely shot away by how minging their ground was compared to Pittodrie, but I was also shocked at how few people had actually turned out to support the home team. What I suppose must have been their mob at the time could be observed directly across the pitch from us. It was a mixture of skins and the like, mostly with some sort of club colours on show and not a big enough number to really be able to put a quote on. Anyway, Aberdeen were having most of the play when suddenly this skin comes on to the pitch and confronts Gordon Strachan. I thought to myself, Wise up, can you believe this min? I had never seen anything like it! There was a bigger reaction to this than the match itself as I recall. The Jute skin got arrested and the quite bland game continued, with an eventual Aberdeen victory.

Outside, as we left the ground, there was already a sparse running battle going on, with the usual missiles being thrown. This included bottles and stones and bits of red building brick and, to my utter amazement, tins of fucking food! Where we had parked our car there were a couple of rundown-looking convenience shops, which must have been done over during the row. In one of the many sweeping charges, I remember the cars getting hit with a new volley of missiles and I heard the shout 'stand, Aberdeen!' and then 'let's do it, Aberdeen!'

Then suddenly I realised I was lying on the ground. I was helped to my feet, stunned. My head was a bit mushy with blood, and I felt a gouge in it at the back, near my crown. As I got myself together, I looked down to see that the offending projectile had been a tin of fucking food. A well-battered tin of Princess peeled plum tomatoes to be precise! A grin spread over my blood-spattered face as I remembered the words to the song, 'In your Dundee slums, you wreck in the bucket for something to eat, you find a dead rat and you think it's a treat, in your Dundee slums.' Then, instead of launching it back at them or taking it home for a souvenir, I just left it where it was, just in case somebody needed a meal. See, we're not all heartless sheep-shagging bastards in Aberdeen, you know! Anyway, that was my day out at piss-smelling Dens Park. Player attacked, boring win, a bit of a chase and then hit by tomatoes!

Another story from a day out in Dundee comes from the mid- to late-80s. Getting the train was always the most enjoyable way to travel to Dundee and by far the quickest. You would always get a team of between 50 and 100 lads on the main train, with a few on the 9.05am football special, including our Under Fives, who scouted out the

Utility haunts in the vicinity of Castle Street and Commercial Street and the hang-outs around the shopping precinct in the city centre. By the time we got to Dundee, somebody would have sussed the state of play. It had become quite a routine really. I would come in on a train from Inverurie with some of the boys, mainly the lads I'd been at school with, picking up more trendies at Dyce, and then in to Aberdeen. Once we got to the station and met up with other lads waiting to travel, it was the usual nods and handshakes. All the familiar faces were ready for the Saturday mission! Again, I knew a lot of these lads from my school days. Because we moved many times when I was young, I managed to get around four different Academies in Aberdeen, including Dyce, Kincorth, Mackie and Inverurie Academy, and had got to know casuals from all of them.

As I said, some would go on ahead, while others would get a bit of breakfast or hit the bar for an appetiser or, more than likely, a livener after the night before. My haunts were either the Belmont or the Star and Garter, but you couldn't get a drink there until 11.00am. At least if you kept close to the station you could start getting oiled and be on the train for normal opening time. Dundee was only just over an hour away by train. By the time we had picked up a few at Portlethen and then the Stonehaven boys got on, the bulk of the day's mob was on board. The usual non-stop banter ensued, with little bursts of conversation going off all over in the carriages that we had taken over. Some of the lads were talking about what they had been up to the night before. Some talked about new clobber they had bought themselves. Most were talking about the last time out in Dundee. All were buzzing with anticipation.

When we pulled up, there were only our own boys at the station to greet us. There were some of the lads who had gone on the early train, including some of the Under Fives, and a couple of carloads of lads who were there to meet the early risers. The older lads were talking about a leaflet one of the boys had found that had obviously been doing the rounds in Jute City. The basic gist was that we were fuck-all, they were trendier than us and that they had something planned for us. We knew that this would be after the match, because as soon as the OB knew we were in their city they would give us an escort. Anyway, it was signed 'Utility No. 1', which we all knew was a fucking joke. Considering that Aberdeen had already done every other mob in Scotland time and time again and that half the lads saw a day out in Dundee as a waste of time, we just took the threat as the usual mouthy bullshit! As we massed near the rail car park, there looked to be a mob about 100-strong. There were Under Fives still dotted about from the station all the way up to the Murraygate, where we would take our usual route up on to Victoria Road and through Hilltown to Dens Park.

In the meantime, we broke down into smaller groups and filtered into the bars nearest the train station and got the beer flowing again, which was just what the doctor ordered. A group of lads also headed into the city to see what Dundee's early numbers had to offer and to have a root around the shops. After about the third or fourth round we heard a bit of shouting going on and some glass getting smashed out on the road just up from our bar. Some young Dundee had put in an appearance, giving it the 'come on then, Aberdeen'. There was a mad surge of bodies as some of the lads rushed to the door, but the Dundee boys had had it on their toes pretty fucking quick. About 20 or so of our lads gave a bit of a chase, but the rest of us settled back down for another beer and to wait for the next train to come in.

We soon heard the sirens going off in the distance, as was always going to be the case. Now the Tayside OB knew we were there and were going to be all over the station. There was no point in breaking out in clusters as we would get picked off and rerouted and, anyway, the OB were never going to allow that to happen. It was agreed that it was best to wait to see what we had on the next train and then deal with the obvious escort from the OB from there. Another couple of pints and, some time after 2.00pm, the train pulled up. There were another 30 to 40 lads on it, and as we grouped we were told that another couple of carloads of nutters were on their way, having set off at the same time as the last train. They would get there just after kick-off.

As everybody piled on to the road from the various bars and we grouped together for the walk to Dens, there were easily between 130 and 140 lads there ready to do the business. With the others that had already gone ahead and the carloads that were coming later, there were going to be 150-plus ASC in the ground. More than enough to do battle with the combined Dundee mob. There were stories buzzing around that some of the Under Fives had run into trouble near Commercial Street and were getting a doing until the lads from our train, who had gone out for a wander, steamed in and gave it right fucking back to them! A couple of the boys got lifted by the police, but the others were herded up the hill to the ground.

As we walked up our side of the road with a police escort on to Victoria Road, we saw some numbers gathering up the road and across from us. They were chanting at us and throwing the odd missile when the OB weren't looking, but there was very little opportunity for action until we got nearer the ground. Suddenly there was a break and a bit of a running skirmish went on right near where I had been 'tomatoed'. We were fucking fed up by now. Every time we tried to break away, we got pulled up by the OB, who were in good numbers themselves. Obviously they too had seen the flier and the warning that was meant for us.

As we gathered in the pit enclosure, the numbers soon massed and we got into full song. 'You ran, you ran!' taunted the lads who had steamed in when the scuffle broke out earlier. 'Aberdeen, Aberdeen, Aberdeen,' sang the boys as loud as possible as we got ourselves psyched up and ready for the kick-off. 'Come on you Reds, come on you Reds,' came the shouts as the whole Aberdeen away support got set to cheer on our team, led by a 150-plus mob of grinning, buzzing nutters. It didn't matter how droll the weather, surroundings or lack of action had been so far – this was it. This was the buzz! The bouncing, the swaying, the singsongs and the piss-take all mixed together to create the fusion of mad emotions that goes through a supporter's head and heart as the battle between their team and your team commences.

For us it was tribal. Our city against their city. Our mob against theirs. After years and years of taking shit from away supporters, Aberdeen now had the best team in Scotland and the trendiest and hardest mob too, and every game was about being Scotland's number one. Out there on the terraces all the different gangs from the city came together as one united fighting force against anybody that wasn't from Aberdeen who wanted to 'come ahead' and 'have a go'. All the previous turf wars involving the likes of the Hilton 'Tongs' or Kinkorth 'Randal', to name but two of the city's gangs, had become a thing of the past. Every game was about being prepared to go to war with another army from another place on the map.

The players came out and were announced on the tannoy to great cheers. And as we sang 'Scotland's number one, Scotland's, Scotland's number one!' it was not just Jim Leighton we were on about! We started to get into a bit of 'one man went to mow' – it was one of our favourite little numbers, because when we got to 'ten men went to mow' the whole mob used to go loco and would start bouncing around like nutters. It was just a big laugh. Something to keep out the cold and keep the spirits up until after the match. But suddenly there was

OB spilling round the track to get in about us, and they started pulling boys out of the pit. Just because we were having a bounce among ourselves and singing a poxy piss-take nursery rhyme. That's how on top it was on the day. Dundee were giving it the 'you're only sheep-shagging bastards' and we were coming back at them with 'you're only glue-sniffing bastards' or 'I'd rather shag a sheep than an arse'. I think we must have scored because the chant stopped and we started bouncing and going loopy. This prompted the OB to get on it again and once again they were in among us. This subdued things a great deal and the lads were pretty quiet compared to the cacophony that was going off earlier.

I can't remember anything else about the game – I can't even remember if we scored again. Like the rest of the lads, I was pissed off that we had been invaded by the OB, who had tried to shut us down and just wanted to get us out of there. As the game ended and our 'minders' dispersed to deal with the flow of human traffic leaving the ground, we started to chant back at the Dundee who had been having a go. We started to leave and banged our hands hard on the boarding at the back of the enclosure and told them, 'Come and have a go if you think you're hard enough!' It was in reply to their faint taunts of Rangers' favourite song every time we ever scored against them: 'You're gonna get your fucking heads kicked in.' The lads were psyching themselves up big time and were seething with rage as we moshed through the narrow, piss-smelling walkway at the back of the pit and then out on to the road.

One of the main faces gave the shout, 'Come on, Aberdeen, let's do these Jute bastards,' and a deafening roar filled the air as it went right off! Immediately we ran straight into their boys – the ones that stood anyway. The missiles were raining down as usual, but this time it was a constant bombardment. Bottles, bricks, coins, coal, anything that they could get their hands on they threw at us. There was a sweep of charges and stand-offs as Aberdeen backed the Dundee mob off. We charged into them again and ended up on some sort of wasteground where we saw that there were a good 70 or so Jutes waiting for us among the demolished remains of some old buildings. And, as the best half of the mob came into their view, they let us have it again with a stream of missiles. This was it; what a fucking battle!

We ran them; they came back. As the bricks and stones came at us from all sides, we stood, for the most part anyway, only backing off enough to get up a head of steam for one massive charge, and then it came. Loads of lads had been hit, in fact one was bleeding quite badly, and that was all the reason we needed. 'Come on, Aberdeen, let's show these cunts what we're made of,' came the shout, and I screamed along with a load of other lads, 'Let's fucking do it!' As they laid down another volley of missiles, we went fucking berserk, charging right into the best of their boys, knocking the stone throwers flying and popping as many runners as we could. Picking up bricks and stones as we ran into them, we launched their ammo right back at them and they scattered. We kept charging them right down on to the road, where the vans and OB were waiting. They had been all around us but nobody had seen them or heard the sirens during the heat of battle. They started cordoning us off into one big group, using their dogs to round the lads up. Some boys were arrested but they backed most of us up against a wall on one side of the road.

Still easily 120-strong and charged up to the max, we tried to break away to get into the stragglers that were trying to taunt us. We knew that a few of their boys would go ahead and try to have something waiting for us as we approached the station. There were a few sways as the lads tried to make a break, but it was not until we got nearer the station that the opportunity came about. The escort had depleted a bit because they had had to go to deal with other trouble, and, as we turned the corner to more missiles, a massive group of lads broke free. 'Come on, Reds' went the cry as we ran the Dundee again. This time there was more running than fighting, and as we got to the station the sirens were heard and the vans and OB turned up to put an end to the day's business. We hoped that there would be another show and a repeat of a mini-battle that had happened previously on the overpass in the station, but not on this day. The OB had had enough of us and made sure that all the lads in cars were out of the area and that every last man was on the next train.

The journey home was a buzz in itself, with everybody talking about their bit in the rumpus or about the actions of certain lads in the crew. All of us were buzzing about the fact that the Utility thought they were going to get a result by pulling some sort of ambush on us, and instead we stood and they ran. Again! It was a good battle, though, and worthy of the visit after all. All we wanted to do now was get home and get a few beers down us. On the train, plans were already under way for the next day out and a battle with another team's mob.

Chapter 9

WAR WITH THE
OLD FIRM

THE CASUALS

Glasgow was always the most visited destination in our season, being home not only to Hampden Park, where many a good result was had both on and off the pitch, but also to our arch enemies in the Old Firm. And let's not forget clashes with that other Glasgow team, Partick Thistle, where a few good rammies were had. One particular cup game was very memorable. Plus there were at least another half-dozen places just a short train journey away from the city centre that had been the scene of other quality days out. There was Morton, Kilmarnock, Airdrie, St Mirren, Clyde and Motherwell. And not just in the league as there were a few cup encounters too. Notably, Airdrie's 'Section B' and St Mirren's 'LSD' – Love

Street Division – had tried to issue early challenges to Aberdeen, along with Motherwell's Saturday Service. There were a lot of leaflets and graffiti about back then, plus sneaky messages in certain papers and magazines too. But when it really came down to it, even on a shit day with only a few of our lads in attendance, Aberdeen could take anyone's best boys. Wanky little mobs got chased all over their own back yards. And that's a fact!

But the Old Firm of Rangers and Celtic were another thing altogether just because of the sheer volume of numbers that they could attract. Even before the whole casual thing started, the fans of the Old Firm had had a problem with Aberdonians. It had always been a hazardous option as an Aberdeen fan paying a visit to Ibrox or Celtic Park. When the league title went to Pittodrie at the start of the 1980s and the Aberdeen Casuals had made their first appearance, the hatred for Aberdeen fans had reached a scary level. They especially hated the 'casuals', as we were simply known back then because we were the only team in Scotland to have dressers turn out among the travelling away support. Even before I became a casual I had seen and been on the receiving end of torrents of abuse and intimidation that the Old Firm support had dished out. So being attacked by them as a casual was nothing new, although it has to be said that their efforts were far more aggressive and had become concentrated mainly upon us whenever we used to travel to Glasgow to see Aberdeen play.

Celtic Park is a very formidable place to visit. In fact, it can be very fucking scary indeed! A huge stadium planted smack bang in the middle of the Catholic east end of Glasgow, it keeps company with the legendary Barras market area, surrounded by cobbled streets, green bus shelters and shops with cages on the windows. It is a place steeped in history and fuelled by sectarian hatred. Just the sort of place you want to come and spend your Saturday afternoons! Not that we gave a fuck about their politics or their sympathies. The same goes for those other fuckers in Govan. They can hate each other in the name of whatever they fucking well like.

We are Aberdeen. We 'stand free'. We love our club and we love our country. We love our clothes and we love the buzz of coming to places like this and having a mental day out. Simple as that! My first few trips to Parkhead would serve as a scary fucking warning of what a dangerous place it would be to come and visit. On one occasion in the freezing cold winter of 1983, a testy, ill-tempered game had proved barren on the goal front, but there was a Celtic player sent off so that was enough to keep us happy. The second visit was in 1984 in the League Cup semi-final second leg, when we lost 1–0. On both occasions I had gone to Glasgow by coach. I never saw any of the aggro before the games, although I know that there was plenty of it on London Road as the lads from the train made their way to the ground.

At one of the games, I believe it was the league encounter, there was non-stop chanting between the Celtic support and the Aberdeen mob. There were attempts by lads from both sets of supporters to break through the barriers to get at each other throughout the game. The Celtic support launched a fair few volleys of missiles at us, including a sherry bottle, a few empty half bottles and gills of whisky, as well as coins, macaroon bars and the like. This was also the occasion of my introduction to the famous golf ball with a nail in it. Bastards!

The cup game was a fucking mental episode. As usual there was an unconvincing temporary barrier in place with a bit of no-man's-land between the rival supporters manned by a few of Strathclyde's gamest OB! They hated games like this one against Aberdeen almost as much as the clashes with the 'Huns'. Just as with those derby games against their Old Firm enemy, the same sectarian anthems were sung by every man jack wearing hoops, and every single Fenian in the ground knew all the words. This was their back yard and they made no bones about letting us know it, right from the word go.

As they started up their 'roamin' in the gloamin' routine, the Aberdeen joined in with our own version of the song which goes 'roamin' in the gloamin with your penis in your hand...' The crowd, with a 35,000-plus advantage in numbers, had already shouted us down at every burst of song and this too was drowned out by the massed green-and-white support. Every time we got a sway on and chanted 'come on you Reds', they came back at us with a chorus of 'fuck off you Reds'. Then they were all at it with a most rousing rendition of 'glory, glory, what a hell of a way to die- ... to die a casual bastard-.'. Over and over again. All the way through the game they adapted their usual barrage of hatred, normally only used on the Huns.

There was a really evil storm brewing now. For most of the people in the ground, football was the last fucking thing on their minds. That went right out of the window as a loud chorus of 'oh no Pope of Rome' to the melody of 'home on the range' set a charge off from the 1,000 or so fuming Tims bulging against the barricade across from us. Likewise, the Aberdeen mob started a surge and boys were lashing out, launching coins and trying to kick the barriers over to get at the Celtic boys who wanted to fight us. Some broke through and the OB started to panic, trying to keep the angry mobs apart and lifting the ones who managed to get into each other. Keeping the battle-hungry fans apart was their main priority now. The rampant and raging chants of 'you're gonna get your fucking heads kicked in' from the hungry Celtic massive seemed to be coming from all sides of the ground now. But the wound-up and ready-to-rock Aberdeen mob responded with 'come and have a go if you think you're hard enough' right back at them. The atmosphere was pure evil.

I can't remember which song did it. It was either the one about Bobby Sands or another about Johnny Doyle (a Celtic player who had been electrocuted). One of these set off a massive surge from the Celtic support in our direction, and suddenly the barriers were down, twisted and kicked aside, and the Tims were right in among us, hitting everything in sight! The Aberdeen lads at the very front got stuck right in and stood their ground and slogged it out but most were backed off by the sheer weight of numbers pouring over the gap. I was crushed against a barrier right in the very thick of it as Aberdeen charged back into the Celtic support and the fighting started moving back towards the buckled fencing. Even the scarfers in the Aberdeen support lent a hand, fuming at the fact that nobody had been safe during the attack. The Celtic fans didn't care who they hit. Two of my friends from the Dyce coach were really badly shaken up. A lassie was badly crushed against one of the barriers in our part of the enclosure right next to me and required hospital treatment back in Aberdeen. Her step-dad, also my friend, was kicked and punched in the back of the head trying to protect her and his missus.

I just lashed out and tried not to fold under the weight pinning us to the barrier. I don't know how long the incident lasted but there were soon floods of OB everywhere. I was shitting myself, I don't mind admitting it, but you somehow find the inner strength. It's primal. It's animal. And you use it to survive. That's the difference between being the predator and the prey! And in this jungle it was definitely needed. I don't remember anything more of the game itself. I know that they won. That's it. It went right off at the back of the enclosure again but I wasn't involved.

We eventually got escorted to our coaches, some of which had had their windows banged through. We were spat on and pushed about and as we were actually getting on the bus some cunt of a Tim scarfer punched a lassie in the mouth. I swore that day that I wouldn't ever return to Parkhead on any supporters' bus to be threatened, abused and treated the way we were and not be able to do something about it. The next time I went back there I would be on a train – with 400-plus other nutters who wouldn't be taking any shit from Celtic!

Chapter 10

GETTING THERE

THE CASUALS

When I first started going away from home to support Aberdeen I always travelled on supporters' club coaches or football special buses. Even when I first turned trendy I still travelled away by coach for a while. It was partly for convenience, both financial and geographical, but also because I didn't know too many lads at the time. It was only after I moved to the sticks, near Inverurie, and got to know a few of the lads there that I started going away by rail. The casuals had always used the train to get about, and soon I was a regular.

I remember getting on for a pound with lads using a Family Rail Card. You could get up to four youths on the train on one of these. Then there was a promotion for free train tickets run by Persil. The amount of these that my ma got together for me to go away was unreal. I paid as a junior, of course, for as long as I could get away with it. There was also the Young Person's Rail Card, which was good for discounted travel. And then there was 'jumping'. I will admit that I have done this many, many times. It's what you do when you don't have the fare, or just want to save what you have for a beer and the match. You could pretty much do Dundee and back without getting collared, most times. Or you could do the old unlocked toilet trick, with the lads keeping a 'man on' for the guard. You'd get a knock from one of the lads when the guard was approaching, and if he checked in the toilet you were hidden behind the door with your feet up on the seat. I knew lads that would hide between the seats or would be in the toilet with their jeans around their feet when the guard knocked – by the time he got back to them they were gone!

There were really endless ways of pulling a skank. Another one was to say that you had got on at Montrose or Dundee or somewhere and to buy a single to Glasgow and then pull the same trick on the way back. It was all right as long as you didn't get the same guard. It just didn't seem worth it to pay the full weight as the amount of times that you would do it and then not get checked was unreal. Then again, when you didn't have a ticket and they got the hump you could end up being kicked off the train or hit with a fine, and they did start doing that to some of the lads. I'm sure it was something like 25 quid,

DAN RIVERS

which in those days was quite a lot of money. It was the same as you would get for pulling the emergency chain to stop the train – which also happened on a few occasions!

As the OB net began to close in on the clashes between rival mobs and they sussed out our usual meeting times, the train got given up for buses and minibuses. This meant that the number of lads travelling got fewer. The bonus was that we could get a surprise go in on occasion but this soon got stamped out too. There was also the nightmare that the opposition's lads would find the bus and trash it or do the windows, which you would be liable to pay for, as was the case with hire cars. There were many occasions when lads have come out only to find their motor has been totalled for them by the opposite mob. Hibs and Hearts were especially good at doing this. By the late 1980s it was back to the train again for some lads and some games, but for specified rucks the bus was still favoured.

Chapter 11

BEACH END MADNESS

THE CASUALS

It wasn't just away days that were good for a rammy. There were times when we would go on a cheeky little mission into the visitors' end at Pittodrie on a match day. Over the years, there have been some right funny days at the Beach End. By the same token, however, there have also been a couple of close calls. The idea was that a few of the lads would try to slip in among the away support and position themselves as discreetly as possible, in as much as you ever could looking like we did, and then when the time was right they would make themselves known! Apart from visits from Rangers and Celtic, there were very few teams that could bring any sort of numbers with them by way of support, and there certainly would not be many trendies. Really, back in the early days, most away mobs consisted of skins. The likes of Motherwell and Dundee always had skins with their support. Then there was Dundee United, Hearts and Hibs. I even remember St Johnstone bringing a busload of supporters once, with a mainly skin contingent among them. But nobody ever really had any 'lads' with them as such.

I remember many occasions when Aberdeen scored and some of our lads stood up in the Beach End and had a bit of a celebration. But as soon as the OB noticed they were straight in and escorted the Aberdeen down to the front and over the wall, or ejected them from the ground. On other occasions, lads just walked right through the away fans and jumped over the wall at the other end to take their seats among our crew. On a few occasions there was a reaction by the visitors. I remember it going off one time when Hearts were at Pittodrie. There was a group of skins with a union jack sat in the middle of the Beach End and they were getting very vocal to the Aberdeen in the South Terrace.

I'm sure that one of their little chants was 'send your casuals, send your casuals, send your casuals over here'. This was greeted with a huge laugh, a wave and an appreciative round of applause. Suddenly there was a corner and Aberdeen scored. As we enjoyed a bounce – well what bounce you could have in a half-full stadium on a cold day by the sea – we watched for a reaction. The Hearts started giving it to us again until there was a sudden shift of bodies as they noticed about a dozen or so

Aberdeen up to the left of them also having a bounce and taking the piss. The skins made a move towards the cluster of Reds, and there was a bit of a stand-off before the OB intervened and the lads got marched down the benches towards the wall. They took their time getting over the benches, giving Hearts a round of applause for getting upset, and we gave them a rapturous welcome as they jumped over the wall and came in among us.

The same thing happened with the Motherwell travelling support one Saturday in the early 1980s. There was a busload or two of them sat in the middle section of the Beach End and about 20 Aberdeen sat on the benches to the left of them next to the wall. It was a pretty dour game from what I remember, but when the breakthrough came for Aberdeen the trendies in the Beach End celebrated it in fine style. This caused the Motherwell support to attack them and a bit of a go went off as they pushed Aberdeen back against the wall. The lads stood their ground, though, as a few punches were thrown and a load of verbal went off between the two groups. The OB intervened and moved the lads down to the wall again and another piss-take result was had. As I remember it, there was a gathering after the game and a tidy wee mob of lads took to the hill to head to the Motherwell coaches near the Beach Boulevard. Before anything could kick off, though, the OB were on top of it and the coaches were loaded up and seen away from the area.

The same sort of thing happened with Dundee and Hearts. The mini-battles in that vicinity in the old days were pretty mental. I remember many occasions when small clusters of lads would try to slip through the scattered line of OB to get into the Rangers and Celtic, who had been giving it heaps inside the ground. That mad buzz of going ahead towards the hordes on the coaches parked on the other side of that hill was all part of a Saturday for us.

My own first experience of a close call doing Beach End madness came one Saturday when Dundee United came to town. I am certain that it was a cup game of some sort, as they had taken a couple of hundred supporters with them. I remember it was a pretty shitty day and they had about half the end and almost filled it. They were spread out, right up to the back, so as to avoid the nasty cross wind and spurts of icy drizzle. I went round to the Beach End with about ten to twelve lads on a mission. There were a couple of Danestone's and Bridge of Dons' finest on board and a few of the Hilton lads, with at least a dozen or so other Aberdeen lads already in among them. As we came through the turnstiles we could see a scuffle going on near the toilets up to the right of us. A couple of the lads were having it with some United mannies. This blew the boys' cover, and the OB were on it in a flash and the Reds got ejected.

As we got to the entrance at the corner of the Beach End where the rest of the Aberdeen were, some of the United came at us and we ended up having a bit of a go. We were doing well until the OB and stewards moved in again, cordoning us off and ushering the visitors back up to the enclosure. We all got ejected from the ground, names were taken and we were threatened that we would be nicked for public order offences if we didn't fuck off home. We made our way off round the corner up towards the hill and met a bunch of United late-comers and scattered them. The next time I visited the Beach End I jumped over the wall with another Aberdeen lad and we thought we had got away with it as we had almost got to our section when we both got nicked. With our arms up our backs, we were marched past the opposition support along the track and up the tunnel where the dressing rooms are to the OB room. We had our names taken and were cautioned and then ejected via the back of the ticket office.

There were many other occasions when we went to look for a piss-take, but, as the casual thing got bigger and bigger and the other teams started to get travelling mobs together, it got harder to get near them without the OB being all over you. It didn't stop us trying, though!

Chapter 12

MANNIE'S HIDINGS

THE CASUALS

Everybody knows that when you go to a game as part of a mob violence is potentially on the agenda. If it goes off, it's a case of 'do or be done'. I've been stabbed and slashed, bottled and bricked, and punched and kicked because of the football. Make no mistake, when your opposite number 'comes ahead', you fucking stand and fight. You don't run. Not if you're part of a crew. If you do, chances are that what you get off your own mob will be ten times worse than any hiding you might have got if you had kept your bottle together and stood your ground. I have seen many a lad get a proper doing for fucking off in the heat of battle. Never mind being sent to Coventry. You may as well go on the lam and move to Alaska!

The fact is that sometimes you are ahead, dishing it out, having it right off and running them ragged, and sometimes you're the one that gets caught. If you're lucky, it's just a slap. Another time it might be worse. However, getting a 'mannie's hiding', that's a totally different deal altogether. What I'm talking about is when you're surrounded, the blows are coming in from all sides and all you can do is try to protect your face. If you're standing up it's a lot worse in some ways, because you can see the silhouettes of the kicks and punches coming in. It's best to lash out as much as you can and hope that you get a break before you catch a 'goodnight nurse', as I nearly did when I got caught bonny one time at a cup match against Celtic in Dundee in the latter part of the 1980s!

Now, if you are already on the deck and you can't kick your way out, then it's the old curl up into a ball job. You know when you're done for. The hope is that you don't get a boot in the nose. Odds are that your balls have already had a toe-end. Being winded and folded up double is one thing, but a proper bang in the nose is just plain nasty. Your head rings like there is an angry ocean in your eardrums, your eyes fill up with water and your breathing gets totally fucked up. Plus your head is spinning and your orientation goes all to fuck so you just can't get your bearings. Then, if it's a proper 'bleeder', your kit gets all marked up as well. I don't know what's more annoying!

I remember coming out of Ibrox once and getting severely popped. There were 'Bears' everywhere, absolutely fucking hundreds of them. Anyway, about ten feet away one of the lads was down, floored by a dozen blows from the immediate attack. I heard him shout, 'Help me, boys, I'm caught,' in the throng of noise and the rain of blows that we were both receiving. Then I heard him say, 'Ah, wise up, min, nae the nose,' and then a crack. I swear I heard it go. Dirty bastards. He was a right fucking mess, but was more bothered about the state of his new Marc O'Polo sweatshirt than the battering he had taken! As more and more OB arrived to break it all up and the police horses blocked the road off, some of the Aberdeen got us out of there. We regrouped and tried to charge again, but the OB presence was massive now and we were heavily escorted away from the Broomloan Road, with horses in tow, all the way to the tube station. I had eggs all over my head and cuts and bruises everywhere, as well as having blood in my piss for days. Now that was a 'mannie's hiding' day!

Chapter 13

UNDER FIVES

THE CASUALS

Although I was just 15 when I became an Aberdeen Casual, I never got the chance to become part of the established 'young crew'. I lived out in the sticks and so wasn't part of any of the school mobs that used to run around the city. Being quite a big lad, by the time I turned 16 I was managing to get served in most places and at the very least could mingle without getting ejected or drawing attention to myself, and because of this I always managed to muscle in among the older lads. I knew all about the young team, though, and it would therefore not be right if there were no mention of the Aberdeen Under Fives.

Every football firm has got their youth team – the little nutters who go out ahead of the main mob scouting for the opposite team's numbers. These are the young lads who are mainly schoolies and won't get served in a boozer, home or away. They are dressers, just like their older counterparts, and some of them are just as game as the main boys. I have seen tidy wee mobs of youngsters taking on groups of much older lads in equal numbers and running them ragged. So much so that on many occasions there has been nothing left for the main firm when they arrive on the scene. Make no bones about it, seeing a mob of 50-plus young trendies marching about is both an impressive and imposing sight, no matter who you think you are!

Their enthusiasm when telling of their escapades is quite something too. Taking an opposite number's scalp is a big deal for anyone, but with some of the Under Fives you feel like it's Christmas. It's like watching excitable teens boasting about their new bikes or even young lads bragging about their conquests with dames – the rants that come as they try to outdo each other with their tales of war are brilliant. I've been sitting in a bar on many occasions, both home and away, when young lads have come bounding up to the table and started to go into one all at once about some contest with another firm's lads. Each of them tries to shout the rest down to get heard first.

I remember this one time, I think it was around 1987 or 1988, when I was sitting drinking in the Belmont and we had Hearts at home in the league. None of the group that I was with was unduly bothered about Hearts turning up with any lads, and nor were we expecting it. They often brought a few coach loads of supporters, but they had been way behind their city rivals Hibs in the trendy stakes, and at the time didn't really take great numbers away with them by train to have a go. Anyway, there were a good few core lads in the boozer and most of us had been having a beer since before noon. Some time after 2.00pm, a couple of young lads came into the pub and went to the back table, where some of the main lads were sitting, and started going into one about how Hearts had brought a few lads with them. Apparently they had been scouting the train station, and a wee mob of away boys had walked out and into the Trinity Centre, on to Union Street, and it had kicked right off. They had run the 'Jambos' across the road on to Union Terrace Gardens. About a dozen of us went up the stairs to be greeted by a similar number of young lads, all shouting about their bit in the ruck. I loved their enthusiasm and the excitement among them. No sense, no fear. Brilliant!

A couple of lads said they would go for a wander with the youngsters to see if there were any strange faces still about, but I remember this lad with a 'tache, who was a bit of a face among the lads, just laughing this dirty, hysterical laugh. He just went to bits. I don't know if he had been popping out of the side door to breathe Morocco with a few of the back table all day or what, but he set the rest of us off in stitches. You know that contagious laughter, where you have no idea why you're laughing but you just can't help yourself. Well, there we were, tears running down our faces, trying to hold it together so as not to give the game away, heading back downstairs into the bar. And one of the lads pipes up and says, totally straight-faced, 'Wise up, boys, it cannae be that bad, can it?' Well, that was it; we all just went to fucking pieces. I know that I laughed so hard that my head was thumping for the rest of the day. I can't remember the game or any subsequent action. I just remember that laugh setting off tears in the eyes of some of the scariest and hardest nutters in the Aberdeen mob.

All laughs aside, a lot of these youths have notched up some pretty big conquests over the years. Setting upon mobs as soon as they have left the train station was always a favourite, or sending the opposite numbers in all directions and then picking them off. Or causing diversions so that the bulk of the mob could move into position elsewhere. I've seen them go ahead into a trouble zone and draw the other firm out, and then the main team has come in behind the opposition mob or steamed in from the side like a military flanking manoeuvre.

It must be said that the Under Fives' absolute favourite is marching ahead in front of the lads, looking out for a target, and then, knowing that they have the backing of the best boys, steaming straight in! I remember seeing them go mental at Celtic. Running right into a mob of mannies and attacking buses as it all went off. Likewise, they have gone ahead at Partick, Clyde, Dundee and Hearts, to name but a few, and especially at Arbroath in the cup when they were pretty fucking impressive to watch. Away from home it is obviously better for them when the main firm is close by. We don't want our Under Fives getting done. Especially as there are a lot of wee brothers playing in the young team. I will say, though, that they have not always come off the best – in fact, some of the young Aberdeen have had pretty good kickings, and there was one time when there was a knifing when the Under Fives paid a visit to Perth one Saturday afternoon. I can assure you, though, the bastards from the very shit Fair City Firm got a visit from some very scary characters within our mob and they gave them a gentle reminder about what a real football crew is all about!

At Pittodrie, though, it's a different thing altogether. It's our manor and we defend it with everything we've got, and the same goes for the young lads. They have been ready, mob-handed, to do the business when Motherwell came to town, and have held their own in some pretty tasty clashes: with Rangers on Union Terrace, Dundee United on Market Street, and Hibs in the Trinity Centre and underneath the stairs near platform 9 at the station. These are some of the times that stand out in my mind. There have also been some pretty mental running battles involving the youth team on and around the hill behind the South Terrace. And maybe this is a good time to remind you all that Aberdeen have never been done at home, and very few visitors have rejoiced in taking a liberty for more than five minutes!

So, while their zeal has been the source of some quality amusement on occasions, the Under Fives do a very important job within the structure of the mob. Every mob needs their juniors, and, as the years have gone by, the lads that have come through the ranks from the Under Fives to being top boys within the mob have all made their mark. Fair play to them!

Chapter 14

PLASTICS, BEAUTS, SPECIALS, TINKS AND MINKERS

THE CASUALS

This is just a little chapter dedicated to those strange and annoying folk that we have had to put up with over the years. Not that they deserve any kind of recognition in any positive sense. These people truly are worthy of the negative backlash they have received and the character assassination that I will now bestow upon them. 'Plastics' are the bastards that can be seen walking the streets at about 5.30pm on a Saturday afternoon, trying to mingle with the post-match flow of human traffic. They dress in what they think is 'trendy' attire, in an effort to look like us, except they have missed the whole fucking point. Not only do they not attend the football or know how to fight, but they also have no fucking idea how to dress. They are fakes in every way.

They're pretty much all 'beauts', or, in plain English, not very attractive folk. They can be seen wearing such good-quality items as Le Shark polo shirts and Leo Gemelli jumpers. They might also be wearing those nasty marbled jeans, and their top trainer could be anything from those garish Asics gels to Adidas Bamba, at a push. For years they have been the fair game of many an irate trendy and with every justification. 'Specials' are those folk that don't look quite right and could easily be the product of wrongdoing between two members of the same family. 'Tinks' are the beauts that could be the spawn of specials. 'Minkers' are along the same lines as tinks. They have no self-respect or sense of style. They can only hope to develop into 'beauts' and finally into 'plastics'. I hope that's clear now!

Chapter 15

HOUSEMARTINS

THE CASUALS

Apart from their clothes and obviously the football, most of the lads that I knew were also bang into their music. There was a vibrant band scene on the go in Aberdeen at the time and also some good Northern Soul nights. Clubbing in the mid- to late-80s, as any of the lads will recall, usually consisted of cheap piss, dodgy dress codes and maybe trying to get a 'trap' to a smoochie number by Culture Club or Spandau Ballet. This would often end in a messy kebab or a row with some beaut and his minging ugly dame while jostling for a cab on the way home!

For the folk that were into their live gigs, there was the Capitol Theatre on Union Street. In that mid- to late-80s period, the bands that were big included the likes of The Smiths, Lloyd Cole and the Commotions, Echo and the Bunnymen and The Fall, to name but a few. Scottish bands that were big included Deacon Blue, Simple Minds and Hue and Cry, but the most memorable gigs for me were by Big Country and Runrig, when they passed out crates of beer and champers to the crowd. At all of these gigs, there was a contingent of football-going lads.

I also remember coming back from a 2–2 draw with Celtic at Parkhead one time with a good team of us going straight from the train to rock the Capitol and bounce to the sounds of The Cult. You'd also get a good-sized crowd of trendies at the Waterboys gigs. At any of these gigs when there was a football element in the house you always got a good noise, and the better the band, the bigger the feedback and audience participation.

The first time that a cheeky little combo called The Housemartins visited Aberdeen was in 1986. They were straight out of Hull, with a fresh face and a punchy sound. With them came a clever anti-establishment attitude with a political undertone, and they looked typically laddish, which meant that their appeal to the football crowd was guaranteed. This was especially the case in the north of England and in Scotland. Their first epic release, 'Flag Day', set the groundwork for their future 'message' tracks. Penning the lyric 'so you thought you'd like to change the world, decided to stage a jumble sale for the poor, for the poor', Paul Heaton and Stan

Cullimore assured themselves a cult following of angry young men from all walks of life in Britain. It followed suit that the football crowd, and especially those within the casual scene who had some interest in politics, would appreciate The Housemartins' style.

The 1986 gig was raw and vibrant and quite well attended. The set, which included future Housemartins landmarks, was appreciated by one and all. The after-party at an Aberdeen hotel saw a certain Mr Norman Cook taking to the decks, spinning hip-hop to the very fortunate crowd at the basement venue, as the band enjoyed the company of some of our very own likely lads. By the summer of that year 'Happy Hour' had achieved a top chart position and was being played at peak times by all the major DJs on every radio station in the land. The popularity of the album *London 0 Hull 4* ensured that, by the time we saw The Housemartins in Aberdeen again, in 1987, everybody knew who they were. Likewise, their following within the casual scene had mushroomed ten-fold. Another band, The Farm, out of Merseyside, had also gained themselves quite a cult following among the football-going lads. How mad would it be, therefore, if both bands were to appear on the same tour? In 1987, we were treated to a marathon gig, with The Housemartins headlining, The Farm in support and The Cornwalls warming it all up!

I got into the Capitol nice and early and had a scout about. I had a good seat, but this means nothing when you are at a live gig, especially in a venue like the Capitol. It's all about getting down the front, in prime position to see the band and have a good bounce! Very few are sit-down affairs and this was definitely not one of those. After a swift drink, while noting the steady flow of punters, I headed into the thick of it all. There were a couple of hundred already in as The Cornwalls finished up a nice little set and we started shouting for The Farm. This was when I started clocking the lads around me. More and more Aberdeen kept appearing and squeezing into the standing throng of bodies right in front of the stage. The Farm played a rocking set and were cordially treated to a set from us too!

The whole front section of the Capitol was now full of Aberdeen Casuals and it had turned into a football gig. There was a section of the Aberdeen mob who were calling themselves the 'Service Crew' at the time, and a favourite football song to the tune of the Bachelors Cup-a-Soup advert was 'nobody kicks the fuck out of you like the Aberdeen Service Crew', although it was still 'Soccer Crew' to most old heads in the mob. This would be followed by 'nah, nah, nah' and the whole song would kick off again. The bouncing was getting more and more manic as yet more lads steamed forward and the size of the mob swelled.

As The Housemartins came on stage the noise was deafening and the buzz was like nothing I had ever experienced, nor encountered since. The chorus of 'Aberdeen, Aberdeen, Aberdeen' was louder than the house PA, and the band were struggling to win us back. By the time they introduced themselves to rapturous noise from the Aberdeen crowd, the Capitol was absolutely jam-packed. I remember Paul Heaton laughing and saying something like 'It's fucking jumping in here tonight!' We broke into shouts for various tracks and they kicked it all off once again.

Then, as the band started rattling through classic tracks such as 'Anxious' and 'Sheep', the bounce got more and more mental, swaying quite dangerously to the right of me. As the crowd tried to gather themselves, the bouncers were pulling people to safety and a few of them got on stage to shake hands with the band – the casuals were taking over the house once again! This time there was no shutting us up. I don't know how many people you could fit into the Capitol. If the theatre was maybe a 500-capacity venue, I would guess that at least half were match-going trendies, and they made a fucking awesome noise. Absolutely unstoppable!

At this point the gig came to a standstill and the band addressed the crowd. We were still singing like loons and bouncing like we had scored a winning cup final goal, so Paul Heaton said, 'So you're the Aberdeen Casuals, are you?' The noise was mental before, but after Heaton's recognition the volume reached the most ear-popping level I'd ever heard in a crowd. You could see he appreciated that this was predominantly a crowd of football lads, and he started talking to us once again. 'So you're the biggest in Scotland, are you?' he said, and the crowd roared and went into song again, swaying madly. 'So what about the other teams then?' he added, and the whole place started booing, whistling and shouting abuse in his direction. It was as if a Dons player had just been felled by one of the opposition. He gave a nervous laugh and came back with, 'So you don't think much of them then?' playing the crowd along wonderfully. He followed it up with, 'So you're the number one then?' and the crowd went ballistic! A lad jumped up on to the stage and gave Stan Cullimore a handshake and an Aberdeen hat. This signalled a load more hats and scarves to be launched on to the stage, proving that this really was 'our' gig. It was easily as much of a buzz as a match day – minus the row.

The football songs rang out loud and proud as Heaton came back again and asked, 'What about Hull City then? That's my team!' The lads roared at him and a chorus of 'Hull City, Hull City, Hull City' rang out, but was soon drowned out with another tumultuous burst of 'Aberdeen, Aberdeen, Aberdeen'. This was followed by a bounce to 'Scotland's number one, Scotland's, Scotland's number one.' The whole band were now wearing Aberdeen hats, and as Heaton challenged, 'Is that us then?' the crowd responded with a deafening 'yeah!' and clapped and whistled madly. I surveyed the mob around me and saw one of the main Aberdeen faces shouting for the song 'We're Not Deep'. Other boys were shouting for various other tracks, all of them crowd favourites.

The concert continued, and the crowd sang along with the band, and the band sang along with us. There was one vibrant rendition after another: 'Caravan Of Love', 'Build' and so on. It really was a very memorable occasion – one of the rare times that you got a chance to take a good look at your mob outside of a match-day situation. All of them as mental and buzzing as they would be bouncing to an away goal, and every one of them having just as brilliant a time. I didn't want the gig to stop. I remember the sinking feeling as the band went off stage and then the buzz as they came back on again and kicked into 'The People Who Grinned Themselves To Death'. I'm sure they did a second encore and then, suddenly, that was it. They applauded us as they left the stage and the noise that the Aberdeen lads and everyone else in the Capitol made spoke volumes for the performance we had just witnessed. What a gig! What a bounce! What a vibe! Absolutely fucking unstoppable!

It was, without doubt, the best gig I have ever been to, even to this day. As we poured out on to the street, the electricity of the crowd flowed out with us, and the condensation on the doors was a sure sign of the sticky, heady atmosphere that we had been immersed in for the last three hours. Soaked, I pulled my 'Five Get Over Excited' T-shirt out of my waist and fumbled for my ticket stub. I came across one of my souvenir badges, which had the logo 'How Can One Million Elvis Fans Be Wrong?' on it. Indeed, how could they? I know that a good few hundred Aberdeen lads definitely weren't either!

Chapter 16

THE FIRM

THE CASUALS

One of the most influential dramatisations depicting football-related violence ever to grace the small screen was an hour-long made-for-television film called *The Firm*. It centred on the build-up to the European Championship in Germany in 1988 and was about a battle between three English firms to see whose 'top boy' would be the one to lead a national firm following England. The film is set in the camp of the Inter City Crew (ICC). Their top boy, Clive 'Bex' Bissell, is a well-dressed professional man with a young family, a new house and a top-of-the-range motor. Just like for a good portion of the lads to come out of the 1980s, the football, and the violence attached to it, provided the buzz that the characters' otherwise comfortable and safe professional lives could not. As far as violence is concerned, the film focused on the extreme end of the hooligan spectrum, with a shocking use of weapons, rather than the casual influence within British, and in particular English, hooliganism. Dealing rather clumsily with the hooligan issue, the film-makers went for the shock tactic, looking at its results on family life, and acknowledging the effects the 'English disease' had on the national game.

It was the first hooligan film I had seen, and, after seeing the way the lads had taken to it, I knew that it had all the hallmarks of being huge. The fact that all the press people who got to see the film first gave it shock reviews ensured the film had that extra edge. A lot of people wanted to ban it, and for many years it was nigh on impossible to obtain a copy. It was one of those films that was recorded and passed around within the circle, if you like. Arguments rage over the issue of a hooligan mentality, but it has to be said that the film appealed to us in the scene, despite its social implications and the scare-mongering tactics it offered, which was typical of media hype merchants. It was one of those films that was meant to serve as a warning of what can happen if you choose to indulge in this course of recreational pleasure. In truth, I think it only proved to glorify the whole hooligan issue, as extreme as some of the scenes were.

I remember there were some nice motors on display and one or two nice items of clobber too. The 1980s attitude of 'money is no problem' and the confidence that this inspired is also prevalent throughout the film. Though it dealt with out-and-out hooligan violence, rather than the influence of the new casual hooligans, the effects were felt far and wide and it definitely caused a ripple within casual culture.

All through the film there is the comparison between the safety of home and family and the danger of the buzz. At one stage they further emphasise the point when Bex's child gets hurt with the Stanley knife he has used to slash Obo, the general from one of the other firms. Although he sees his car vandalised, his boys slashed and then back out on him, and his home life in tatters, Bex still feels the need to make his mark, and he pursues the Yeti, the final general in the conflict. At best his actions could lead to the loss of his liberty. At worst, the loss of his life! The final scene of the film shows the six remaining ICC lads steaming into the Buccaneers' base-camp boozer armed with bats and doing the Yeti and his firm. But before he has the chance to savour the victory, Bex is shot and killed by the Yeti.

It closes with all the members of the different firms giving an interview to a camera crew prior to the European Championship. Like all good films about gang-related violence and one-upmanship, as well as having the appeal of physical action, it left us with many slogans that would be mimicked by football-going lads across the country for many years to come. The most famous of these being: 'We come in peace; we leave you in pieces!' *The Firm* was one of those films that ended up in lads' video collections along with the likes of *The Warriors* and other gang-related films. I watched it many times as part of the warm-up or come-down from the football. The content has stayed with me ever since!

Chapter 17

ROBBED BY THE TIMS AT DENS

THE CASUALS

As I've already said, you always got a good rammy in Dundee. Granted, a lot of it was running, and mostly us after them, but a battle of sorts was always guaranteed! We had had a couple of mental days out in the cup, two seasons on the trot, against Dundee United in the semi-finals and Dundee in a quarter-final clash. Of course, the two teams' lads pool together to form the Utility, and I've seen them get their numbers up to 200 or so for a special occasion. Anybody who has experienced mob on mob warfare knows the buzz when it all goes off. Being in among it all when 500–600 people are involved in a battle is quite an overwhelming feeling. It just carries you right off.

Now, as much as I hate to admit it and have to accept it, the support that the Old Firm carries is legend. At any game, anywhere, on any day of the week, they can easily muster a travelling support of 10,000-plus. Easily. I don't like it, but we have to face the facts. Surprisingly, they took their time with the formation of mobs of trendies. As I've said, Motherwell's Saturday Service were way ahead of everybody in the Glasgow catchment area and, indeed, ahead of all the other mobs in Scotland apart from Aberdeen.

Of the two Old Firm teams, Rangers would have the bigger mob. Rangers, however, have had to rely on their connection with their English counterparts Chelsea and the use of another English firm's name to help their reputation along. In truth, though, they are capable of pulling good numbers anyway, which is only right to mention, but that is all I have to say about them.

The Tims have got a token show of trendies considering the size of the club. The problem for the Celtic Soccer Crew (CSC) is that their own fans have hated casuals with venomous passion for years and years. They despise us. The battles we have had with mannies in scarves and hoops are legendary. Now, imagine being in Celtic Park among 50,000 fanatical Celtic fans, with maybe 200 or so of you being casuals but also supporting Celtic. There are 49,800 people in the ground wanting to kick your bastard in every time you show up to a game! This is without the other team's lads coming for you too! Not very nice at all, but it's tough shit really. Now they know what it's been like for us all these years, having them singing 'glory, glory what a hell of a way to die, to die a casual bastard' at you at every opportunity. And who can forget that old favourite: 'if you hate the casual bastards clap your hands'? The whole ground gets behind it, clapping like fury and aiming their hate at you! Battles with the Celtic mob have been few and far between. Like most of the other mobs in the Premier League, they were not regarded as serious contenders for top spot, and when previously challenged they had not fared very well at all.

On a cold and miserable night in February 1987, Aberdeen were to play at Dens Park, Dundee, against Celtic, in a Scottish Cup replay. There was always the chance the CSC could put on a bit of a show, or perhaps the Utility boys might have a little reception party waiting for us somewhere along the line. We were buzzing with anticipation at the prospect of both!

My own plans for the trip to Dundee were nearly scuppered by a no-show in the bank of my pay cheque. The plan was to meet some of the chaps for a daytime beer and maybe get a nice new top or something to wear, and then be at the rail bar for teatime. Like I say, though, that went 'oot the windae' and I was left scratching around for the money to get out of Kemnay. I managed to get the bus fare into the city together and then had to go on the 'mooch' among the boys. I didn't like not being flush – I wasn't used to it – but when I managed to get a 'tap' of a score, I jumped at the chance. Then, somehow, I managed to fuck up and nearly blow it again by getting the beers in with a few of the lads. This left me chasing around after my stepdad, who was a cabbie, for another ten spot.

Because of this new complication, I went and missed the fucking train and only by a whisker too! I was thinking to myself, Wise up, min, something's trying to stop me fae getting to this game the day. Freaked out, with my hands pulling at my hair and going into one, I was suddenly grabbed by two lads who said, 'If you hurry up, min, there's still a special over at the bus station.' What a fucking absolute godsend! We were the last folk to be allowed on the last of the five double-decker football specials going to Dundee for the game. The fact that I was bursting for a piss was just tough shit. I had my ticket and I was finally on my way to the match and that is all that mattered. Aye, I was gutted that I wasn't with the rest of the mob – it was all part of the day out travelling with your crew, buzzing each other up, but I knew I would get a bounce and at least be there, and maybe there would be something in store after the match. Considering the cock-up of a day so far, I was thankful for small mercies.

I ended up on the top deck, sitting in the single seat at the front, near the top of the stairs. I think it took us just over an hour and a half and then we were there, 100 yards from the enclosure housing the Aberdeen fans for the night and the pit that had seen many a visit in the past. As soon as we got to the gates I could hear the boys in full song. I went for a 'paddle' in the khazis and then mingled in among the mob in the pit, to the left of the lower-enclosure entrance. At long last I was where I belonged again and I was buzzing.

After explaining for the umpteenth time where I had been, it was time to get into the swing of it. As we roared our team on and went into a mental chorus of 'Aberdeen, Aberdeen, Aberdeen', I surveyed the ground around me. There were Celtic supporters everywhere I turned. They were rammed tight into the end behind the goal left of us and they were also in the upper tier of the enclosure above us and directly across the pitch from us. The place was absolutely jam-packed to the rafters. Aberdeen had a very large travelling support on the day, too, filling out the rest of the ground, and the Aberdeen mob itself looked to be easy 250- to 300-strong!

It was a bad playing surface, which contributed to the slippy, sloppy game in progress, but both sets of supporters kept trying to rouse their respective teams as the atmosphere bordered on tedium at times. Celtic went close and set the hordes in green and white off on one again. First it was a bit of 'soldiers are we', followed by a faithful rendition of 'roamin' in the gloamin'. We duly obliged by 'baaing' at them, giving them a round of applause for their efforts and hit back at them with some 'northern lights of old Aberdeen' and our other proud anthem 'stand free'. It seemed like a non-stop sing-athon, with both factions baying to drown each other out, though, in truth, there really was very little to sing or get excited about. The game was a very scrappy affair with not a lot in it, and the bastard in the black was playing his own

Aberdeen vs Rangers at Ibrox in 1985.

An Aberdeen crowd in 1987.

Aberdeen vs Rangers in May 1987 at the Pittodrie.

part in it all, with some very debatable decisions indeed.

Half-time came and went, with more visits to the trenches and catch-up discussions in full flow, and, before we knew it, the teams were back on the park and the game was back in play. We had had some shit off the Tims above us in the stand at half-time, so the hostilities on the park were shared with the green-and-white bastards in our midst. We bounced about and swayed angrily as the play became more and more frustrating, urging the team on. We started letting fly with some war cries: 'We're Red, you're dead, we're bouncing on your head, we're Aberdeen, we're Aberdeen!' They of course came back at us with their 'hail, hail, the Celts are here' anthem and all the hoops got into it in unison and then followed it with one of their own special war cries. We hated this and all the bigoted religious shite they were used to using on the Rangers. It had nothing at all to do with this game or with us.

We were in the middle of another chorus when suddenly the ground went ballistic. One of the players had done a weaving little manoeuvre into the box and had dropped like a fly as soon as he was challenged to the deafening roar of the Celtic support. The red-and-white half of the ground went equally mental, crying down the decision, as the referee pointed to the spot. If there were a footballers' diving competition on offer at the Olympics, the Old Firm players would win gold medals every fucking time, without doubt! The violence in the air among the boys in the pit now was unbelievable. Our hearts were in our mouths as we watched, and, for a brief second there as the penalty was stroked in, it was like my ears had popped. Then suddenly it all went off! The whole place was rocking. The Tims were bouncing like fuck, jubilantly rubbing our noses in it, yet again. The bang and clatter of the Celtic fans jumping in the upper level of the enclosure to our backs was a heart-stopper in itself.

All around the right side of the stadium every single Dons fan was booing and going bloody mad and the whole Aberdeen mob went absolutely fucking bananas. I can't think of many more times where I have seen them go so daft in a ground. One of Aberdeen's main faces and another favourite character of mine just went absolutely light! He was so incensed with rage that he was trying to climb the wall to get into the bastards that were behind and above us. They were blessing us and spitting down on us and giving it the big one. I thought that one of them had poured a drink down on to us but one of the lads said that we were being pissed on. Why we never invaded the pitch there and then, I will never know.

I can't remember anything else of what was left of the game. We just went fucking loopy and I'm sure we made to leave the ground pretty soon after the goal, launching handfuls of coins and anything we had into the Celtic support above as we left. We banged that hard on the boarding near the cesspit toilets and roared that loud with collective rage that it sounded like an earthquake. The echo of the angry stampede made my head ring. As we broke out on to the road there were bodies scattering everywhere. I think that everyone in our way was flattened! Tims, Jutes – it didn't matter to us. We went steaming down this road where there was a show of Celtic who wanted to have a go and they got flattened too.

I made the mistake of getting too carried away, wading in as we charged through the group, and fell back in the mob. The Celtic now swarmed in to have a go at the last few Aberdeen boys. As I was fighting away, I turned to look for back-up but there wasn't any. Then a punch came in off this big Celtic mannie in a hoop top and scarf. He caught me right off the side of my head, sending me reeling. I then caught kicks and punches from all over the place as I was backed up against a fence, with dozens of Celtic running to pile into me.

The Tims that the Aberdeen mob had steamed into were now aware that at least one had been caught and were all coming to have a piece. Blow after blow came in. I must have taken 60 or 70 hits to my face, head and body, when this lad in a black leather bomber jacket – I think he was a trendy – stepped into the fray, swinging me sideways off the fencing. As more hits came in and a few of the Tim mannies were breaking up the fence posts to finish me off, he pulled me away again saying, 'You better fucking run; they're going to kill you!' and sent me in the direction of the hill that the Aberdeen mob had raced up, leaving a trail of destruction in their wake. Cars, windows – everything got it that night! As I looked back, I could see him trying to run, taking punches as he did so. This was a Celtic casual. He risked his neck to save mine, despite all the politics of inter-mob warfare. I owe him for that and I will never forget it as long as I live!

I ran like the wind to catch up with the mob and did so. As we turned this corner, a load of missiles rained down on us, including bottles and stones. This one lad ran out into the road and went to launch a big glass juice bottle, like the Bon Accord ones we have in Aberdeen, and he somehow slipped and landed on it. The Aberdeen mob were on him and his mates like a swarm and he got steamed good and proper. I will never forget him screaming out loud in pain. It turned my stomach, and I had a flashback to March 1985 and the battle on Easter Road with Hibs. I don't know how that lad fared but I bet he was in a pretty bad state.

There was no more opposition all the way to the station, and before I knew it I was on the train. Sat across from me was one of my old-school ASC pals and one of the twins I had been to school with. Another of the Inverurie lads who was sat with us had ripped his jeans in battle, and they were all concerned for the other twin, who was missing. None of us got checked on the train on the journey back for a ticket, which was just as well as I had gone there on a bus and barely had enough for the fare back. Mad chatter was going off all over the carriage about the fight with Celtic outside the ground. I had my own tale to tell about that one. I hurt from head to toe but would never let on how done-in I felt. I could still see the bastards wading into me in my mind's eye.

When we finally arrived in Aberdeen after a very

sombre journey, I stuck with the Inverurie lads. After ringing around a bit to try to ascertain the whereabouts of the missing twin, a lift was arranged and an hour or so later we were picked up. They were good enough to drop me off in Kemnay on their way to Inverurie, thank fuck. I got into my ma's and sat down and took it all in. It seemed like something was trying to stop me from going to Dundee, but no, I wouldn't have it, would I? No matter what, I had to be there, end of story. It was nearly my lot, though, and, as the bruises came out over the next week or so, I questioned myself many, many times. I can only put it down to it being in the blood, and the following Saturday there I was in my seat at Pittodrie, with the lads all around me, once again singing 'come on you Reds!'

Chapter 18

BUS TO OBLIVION

THE CASUALS

Ever since the incident in March 1985 when the Hibs lad had got really badly hurt, the war with their crew had got right out of hand and had become very scary indeed. On the next few meetings the Capital City Service had made their point good and proper that the events of that day would not be repeated. They had thrown a petrol bomb at the Aberdeen mob as they came up Princes Street later that year, and had also fired a shipping flare at Aberdeen on another occasion. I remember being told by a lad that on one occasion, as the Aberdeen mob were pulling into Waverley, there were a load of Hibs lads waiting at the station. He barely had a foot on the platform when he got popped on the nose. It had literally gone off the minute Aberdeen had arrived, such was the rivalry between the two mobs.

I missed out on a fair bit of the action in 1987 and 1988 as I had taken a management job. I had on occasion let my Saturday afternoon shenanigans get in the way of my work. Luckily for me, I escaped serious disciplinary action because one of my district managers was an old-school Aberdeen Soccer Casual. He had been the one behind the 'EVEN RAMBO RUNS FROM ASC' banner at Hampden in 1985. As he stood there in his Hugo Boss suit, his look completed with a back-perm, I knew I was getting away lightly and that my hooligan boss would not be there for me the next time. So, when the opportunity came about for a better-paid job elsewhere with another company, I took it. Unfortunately, this meant working and living in Edinburgh, so, for safety sake and the sake of my job, I left my casual antics alone for a while.

I still kept my ear to the ground, though, and was made well aware that Hibs had taken the piss by stabbing an Aberdeen lad outside the Beach End in late 1987. This had led to a major retaliation plan in which Aberdeen had taken possibly their largest away mob, bar cup final business, to the next away fixture at Easter Road in early 1988. Some 600-plus lads were pooled together to seek revenge and wreak havoc on Edinburgh, but a massive OB operation put paid to most of the day's violence. The train journeys were getting too difficult because of OB intelligence, and instead the lads were going away by bus. There had already been a visit to Easter Road that had resulted in one of the coach windows being banged through as the Aberdeen mob's bus was heading up Princes Street. Another occasion saw the whole Hibs mob emptying out of a bar near the bus station and steaming straight into the two busloads of Aberdeen as they gathered on arrival in the capital. Sadly three of the boys present on that day are no longer with us. With one thing or another, the numbers going away had dwindled and only the nuttiest bunch of loons would get a bus together to go to the likes of Hibs.

On this occasion, in the late summer of 1988, there was a match on a Tuesday or Wednesday evening. I had not been into Aberdeen for a while and had not had a beer with my old best mucker from Danestone in that time. I caught the early bus in and met my man at Littlewoods. I think that when two 'lads' meet up at 11.00am, it can in all honesty only lead to a visit to the pub. I can't remember if we had a scout about for clobber or not that day. For sure, not long after hitting the city, the first golden drop of the day was slipping down nicely in the Star and Garter bar. One pint followed another, and we ended up going for a wander. I'm sure that we gorged our way through a couple of shepherds and beans at the baker on Belmont Street, and then headed into one of our favourite bars next door, the Belmont.

A couple of the better-known chaps were in there, and as we sat with a fresh pint the subject of the match was broached. I had kept it to myself that I'd heard about a bus going from the art college and waited to see if he was up for it or not. We both pissed ourselves laughing, as it turned out that he was waiting for me to bring the subject up. There was a nervous expectant silence between us for a moment, but it seemed like ages. I told him to get a round in while I hit the khazi, and when I returned I said, 'Well then?' He just said 'well' in reply, so I retorted, 'Are we gan te dee it then or nae?'

'May as well,' came the response, and we just laughed and both said, 'For the fun of it!' at the same time. This is what it had always been about for the two of us.

As the beer flowed and we got closer and closer to the departure time, it was like we were waiting for the other one to make the first move. The lads we had seen in the bar had been gone a while now. I don't know if my man was reconsidering the idea or if he was wondering about my own intentions. With the recent history between the two mobs, it was sure to be a fucking mental deal, one way or another! Finally, I made the move to the door and ten minutes later we were at the top of the street, feeling pretty heady, with six or seven pints in us each. This was the only bus and it would have to be full of mental bastards to be leaving at four in the afternoon. Right enough, it was, and I was privileged to be one of them. My mate and I took our seats on the right as you got on, about three rows back from the front. After we started to pull away, a lad came round and collected the pitch-in off all the boys aboard this bus to oblivion.

This was it; we were off. There was no backing out now and neither would we want to. Make no mistake, we knew what we were here for. It felt like we were part of the elite. It always did. There were very few people who would be accepted on a bus with this lot, I can tell you, and there would be a hell of a lot more who wouldn't thank you for the chance! The hardcore loons were at the back, as per usual, and everybody else on the bus made sporadic conversation. I really can't remember very much more about the journey after leaving the city. I just know there was a tension you could cut with a knife as we entered Edinburgh.

It was important to be aware of your enemy and their capabilities. I suppose you could call it respect. I know I still had that 'healthy respect for my work' feeling that the old-school Aberdeen lad had talked about, all those years ago. I could see that some of the other lads had that feeling too, but some lads didn't give a fuck! Granted, this was a scary place to come, and Hibs had some mental bastards in their mob, but no more mental than our lads. This was Aberdeen, and I had been all over the place with these boys and trusted them with my back 110 per cent. We wouldn't be here on a night like this if we didn't all think the same about each other. As we pulled into the bus station after a tour of Princes Street, we were ready to go. All 50 Aberdeen!

We came out of the station, with there still being no sign of Hibs. They had also been absent from Princes Street. We knew they would be ready and waiting for us, though, and as we came off Leith Street into Leith Walk they let us have it! I didn't hear a fucking thing; that's what did me.

Then suddenly I was unconsciously moving forward and there was a clash of bodies. Fucking loads of CCS had rolled down the grass embankment to our right-hand side and hit us hard from all angles. My mate had been off his mark like a bolt of lightning as he and a few other Aberdeen had made a move to steam in. I can't even remember landing a hit but I took one to the belly and also my back.

Then suddenly the action ceased and the OB were in the middle of the road with a couple of vans. They had nicked my mate and one of the main Aberdeen faces. I remember one of our lads had smashed his watch – I think it was a Tag – sending one of the Hibs flying over the bonnet of a car. It was some punch, I can tell you. I'm not sure but I think he may also have been nicked. We were down to about 45 or so lads when the OB ushered us together and sent us on our way. The Hibs were put in the opposite direction, but some tried to ghost it down the road opposite us.

As we approached the narrow bridge, one of the Aberdeen's main faces and a favourite character of mine told us, 'All you boys better stand, especially you Tilly boys.' He was clearly fucking fuming at the ambush back up the road – we all were. There was no more opposition as we approached the ground. I can clearly remember the OB taking pictures of us with a huge telephoto lens as we made to pay our way in. There was a half-decent travelling support down from Aberdeen, and a few lads were already there with more on the way. I had been bursting for a piss since just after Dundee and went to find a bog pretty quick. It was a pretty mental piss I can tell you, and I was worried I'd had a drip as my pocket was damp. But it wasn't piss – it was blood, and I discovered a token slice just above my pelvis, maybe big enough to put a fingertip into. I never felt a fucking thing. The adrenalin must have been pumping that madly. I was more bothered about the pain in my back. I'd taken a beating on a few occasions and the kidneys never did take too well to it.

I went to have a word with the OB to see if I could visit the first aid people. I just wanted a clean and patch-up job and the all-clear so I could get back to my crew. I remember as I was led round the track to the tunnel the Hibs supporters hissed and spat at me. Fucking bastards! I was asked by the paramedics what the matter was and to take off my shirt. When they saw me they weren't happy about letting me go with a clean-up job, insisting that whatever cut me might have fragmented inside me. I would need an X-ray and maybe a tetanus jab and my kidneys looked at. It was ridiculous, all this over an incident that happened in the blink of an eye. I don't mind telling you I was shitting myself as they put me in the ambulance and some of the Hibs boys peered round the doors to see whose boy was inside. One of them shouted something like, 'I hope ye die, ye bastard!' as they shut the doors and drove off to the infirmary.

That was one of the scariest nights of my life. Sad to admit it, but it's true. Here I was, an Aberdeen Casual and the arch enemy, in an Edinburgh hospital with no other

Aberdeen lads in plain sight and quite a few Hibs in there at the hands of my mob. It was nasty, I can tell you. There were CCS boys walking about the cubicles, nosing around at who was in and for what, while the OB stood watch. After the game, which Aberdeen won, there had been another battle and Aberdeen had given a good account of themselves, sending a few more Hibs boys into the casualty department and leaving me in the wrong fucking city to deal with the consequences. Luckily for me, the dame I was seeing at the time managed to convince her old dear into coming and getting me from the hospital. I was in there for nigh on seven hours! By the time she arrived I was just about worn to a frazzle, having had to satisfy the doctors and OB of what had happened, and having to dodge the Hibs lads that were there all night.

The lads that were nicked appeared in court the following Monday and were bailed to appear at a later date. The dressings helped the nick heal; in truth, it was just a surface wound and the bruise from the jab quickly faded. But the tales from that night were told for a long time after and now you've read mine!

That was my last day out to Hibs with the lads. In fact, I stayed away from the football for a wee while after that, never really letting on to anyone, apart from a few very close friends, about my own tale from that night. The way I saw it, the caper had changed too much and, yes, if I'm honest, I got a scare. I know lads that felt the same way as I did, especially after the petrol bomb and flare incidents. It seemed like the game had turned into guerrilla warfare and that just wasn't what it was about for me. I was in it for the crack, the day out. Getting dressed and the meeting up and the beers and the buzz of the camaraderie and maybe a set-to, if anyone came ahead.

I was ready and willing and plenty able to do the necessary when it came down to it but all this weapons shit was bollocks. All the time I was with Aberdeen, nobody ever got tooled up for the day out. It was hands, head and feet and that was plenty good enough. What happened that day, though, left me with a bitter taste in my mouth. A few of the lads present on that night were left feeling shot away too.

However, it was in the blood and I did return to the football and tried to recapture that thirst for the 'day out' I knew and loved. Just as any football lad will know, that feeling you get out of the caper, it's just too good to let it alone for too long.

Chapter 19

THE GLORY WALK

THE CASUALS

There is a place that, for the sake of giving it a name, I shall simply call the 'glory walk'. The 'glory walk' is the area in Aberdeen that I observed for many years and regarded as the place to be. It was the place to be seen, where absolutely anything could happen, and on a match day it was a living, breathing action cinema.

In truth, the 'glory walk' could really encompass the whole area between the Holburn Street end of Union Street and Pittodrie Stadium itself. But the main focus that I'm going to talk about is the Union Street zone between Holburn Street and King Street. On a Saturday from early doors, this main city street is a throng of buzzing activity. It starts at opening time, when hundreds of bodies pile off buses and into the shops or emerge from the railway station and enter the Trinity Centre to spend their hard-earned cash. There are thousands of bodies everywhere, and the numbers only get larger when the central city bars open their doors and the match-going lads savour their first pint in their regular haunts.

If you lived 'out the road', as many of the football lads did, it would mean a very early start for your journey by bus, taxi or train. And, if it was a proper day out, that was really par for the course. When I first turned trendy I was staying 'right out the road', and it was an hour-and-a-half coach journey into the city – and that was always at the mercy of the bastard driver on the day. I was staying on a main bend on the A96 Aberdeen to Inverness carriageway, about 100 yards from a village where there were about ten houses, a shop-cum-post office and a sawmill. It was very quaint and full of old-world charm, but a right fucking pain when it came to matters of commuting. If the bus driver saw you or could be bothered to stop, you were on your way. If not, you were pretty much fucked. So there was this coach or you could stump up for a taxi, otherwise it meant walking the six-mile journey to Insch. From there, there was the possibility of yet another local bus or the train.

A very good friend of mine at the time was one of *the* trendiest guys I had seen in the casual scene up until that point. He was an executive officer in the civil service and lived out that way and swore by the train out of Insch, so it became the favoured mode of travel into Aberdeen for a match day. Before long, having shared a few days out together, I came to know the Inverurie and Kintore boys who also did the football, and this would always be the start of any proper day out. However we got there, we would arrive in Aberdeen city centre nice and early. If it was by coach, then it was usually about 9.35am on Union Terrace Gardens, traffic and conditions permitting. If it was a train job, then it was into the city within ten minutes either side of the bus. Sometimes we'd have a breakfast beer in the station area and then have a wander and a root round the shops until opening time, but on away days it was really a case of getting there and staying close to the train station.

Always, though, right from the start of the day, there were casuals to be seen all over the place, but especially within the 'glory walk' area. There were the keeners, who were just as sick as I was in those early days, all in a state about the game and the possible foe at hand. After a sleepless night, you would be up at a ridiculous time sorting out the right gear for the day. Then, dressed and ready to rock, you would be in the city at some stupid fucking time, searching out your own kind. I know that that is how it was for me. As the human traffic multiplied and the city started to buzz, those like-minded individuals from my crew would gather together and start putting themselves about and scout out for signs of the enemy. A fellow old-school Aberdeen lad from those days used to call this match-day parade and hunt scenario 'walking the matt'. And it really was like that, walking up and down the

street and back and forth across the road over and over
again – all the time trying to look casual, but at the same
time trying not to look bang on top. This was a
contradiction in terms, I felt, but there was always some
kind of action or incident on the 'glory walk'.

I remember vividly this mad hive of activity as the day
approached noon. You had the graveyard in the centre of
Union Street, where the young city trendies would hang
about and where a good number of the buses from all
over would stop and empty. Then there was the junction
of Bridge Street and Union Street, where C&A was. This
used to be a big meeting place – not for trendies as such
but more so for schoolies, couples, shoppers and so on.
Then there was Wimpy, but again that was mainly for
schoolies and fresh Under Fives and not really a place to
be seen as they had security cameras even in the early
1980s. Then there was Littlewoods, which was on the
other side of the Trinity Centre entrance, with Pizza Hut
and a shoe shop. You would still get boys who would hook
up there in odd wee numbers, but this was the central belt
and the core of the city so it was far too on-top to be seen
in any numbers as you had store detectives and OB on
your case straight off, and that was no good to anybody.

It was around this area that most of the sport on a
match day used to happen. You had Union Terrace
Gardens across from you and the Trinity Centre and train
station behind you, and it seemed like everything
happened in this bit of space on the street. Depending on
the time of day and the foe that was in town, this was how

you marked your position. I have been stood at the entrance of Littlewoods a few times when all hell has broken loose on Union Street. There have been boys running about and shouts going off and it has been funny as fuck to watch.

I remember one time, probably about 1987, when I was stood at the main doors, eating a buttery and sipping a hot coffee, and on the other side of the door was one of the main faces in the Aberdeen mob at the time. He was a very smooth-looking customer indeed. Some lads had spilled out of the Trinity Centre on to Union Street, obviously in battle with whoever the foe were for the day – I think it was Hibs. These lads were causing a right commotion and bringing it on top, and I caught this senior Red's eye and we just laughed about it. He shook his head, pulled a sandwich out of his pocket and stood there eating it, cool as a cucumber. The row came within feet of us and we just watched them getting all excited and carried on as normal. It was brilliant.

Then there was the time when I was involved in a beef outside Littlewoods that spilled into the store, and when the OB turned up everyone just scattered. I was up the escalator and in the posh café queue with sweat pouring down my face, but when the OB poked their head in I was ordering a mince pie and a pot of tea, my Burberry scarf stuffed up my denim jacket. Another time I was hidden in the homewares department as they were nicking boys for the fracas at the front of the store.

I also remember seeing wee groups of young trendies

going up to different people and giving them the hard-man routine, totally off the wall. 'Are you Aberdeen, like?' but in the full Aberdonian accent. This was a practice that would be adopted by many an up-and-coming lad out headhunting an opposition foe's scalp. I have been caught a few times myself by these scary wee lads. One time I was in the city nice and early for the Tims at home and had met a few of the boys and had a root around the shops before going straight into the Belmont for early beers.

At some point in the proceedings I went into the wee John Menzies newsagent on Union Street to get a paper and some munchies, and as I jostled in the queue I clocked a group of about five young nutters gathered outside the shop window giving me the eye. I knew that they weren't Celtic, because what trendies Celtic did have would never have travelled to Aberdeen, let alone be stood outside a busy Union Street shop in the city centre looking decidedly dodgy! I could tell that they were drawing lots for who was going to come ahead with me first, and really it was down to whichever one of them had the bottle to do it. I knew how that felt, having gone through the motions of the challenge myself, and even though the quandary had its amusing side I had to respect that they were out to make their mark and that I may well have to steam into them if need be.

I came out of the shop and copped a glance at them still in front of the window to the left of me, and I made to the right towards the Belmont again, keeping an eye on them trying to case me. I got about ten to fifteen feet down the road and I could hear them cantering up behind me, one of them shouting after another, 'Tell him who we are.'

It was fucking priceless! I swung round and challenged the closest youth. 'What's the fucking crack then, you dicks?' I screamed.

One of them came back, 'Do you ken far we are, like?'

I went, 'Who the fuck are you, like?'

And, as they got their hype ready, one of them went, 'We're Aberdeen, who are you?'

Well, as much as I was dying to burst out laughing right at that very point, I just let them have it nice and firm, 'No you're nae, boys, I'm Aberdeen and I don't know who the fuck you think ye are, but you're way out of your league here!' The look on their faces was fucking brilliant, and, before they could get any more courage up to give me any further verbal, I told them, 'You better fucking come round the boozer and tell this to the boys, you fucking tubes.' This finished them off nicely and then I recognised one of them as the wee brother of one of the city faces, who also happened to be in the Belmont with me and about 25 other lads. He declined my offer and I told him, 'The boys you want have got fucking stripes on. If you see any of them, you better make a better job than you did with me!' Laughing, I made my way to the boozer and watched the youngsters skulk off in search of a better mark.

As I have said, the living cinema consisted of thousands of shoppers and commuters, but there was also the unmistakable sight of the trendy-looking chaps out on parade. All over the place, as far as the eye could see, there were little groups of lads, weaving in and out of the normal shoppers, dressed and on the hunt. The idea of course was not to get noticed as such by the OB, but they clocked everything that was going on and you could be sure that, if anything kicked off on the 'glory walk', there would be a hundred different witnesses that saw the whole thing! Many a lad has been pulled up for something that he didn't do or for being an active part of a deal that went down when in fact he was just a passenger. There were so many different little actions going off all over the place that you could never fully appreciate it in its full 'glory'.

There's one final memory from the 'glory walk' that is certainly worthy of mention. I was with a very good friend and fellow Red from Danestone and we had been having a few drinks. We must have been playing someone shite away from home, and, whoever it was, most of the ASC nutters that I knew had been seen in and around the city at some point and we'd been drinking with a good few of them for the better part of the day. Anyway, something had popped in the Star and Garter and there was some row between a few of the lads and some Irish fellas and the whole day was fucked. There was an evil atmosphere in the pub after that, as some of the boys had fallen out among themselves.

This sort of shit always did put my back up. I had had to deal with a nasty one between some Aberdeen the week before. I had been on the piss all day with some boys from

Newtonhill and one of the Stoney nutters was trying to kick off with one of them. It was one of those pissed-up, blurred brawling and swaying around jobs, like some mad paralytic rugby scrum. A few punches and kicks were thrown and there was loads of pointing going on. The row was over this Newtonhill boy getting off with the Stoney lad's dame on a few occasions and this lad wanting closure on the matter. The night was fucked and the numbers dwindled and I appeased the OB with my 'calm head of reason' routine and put the Newtonhill lads in a cab and saw them all home.

When we got back a row had broken out with the lads in the cab, who were all fuming at the geezer concerned for winding up the other Red and for fucking the session up. So I asked him, 'What was all this really about, min?' and he came back saying, 'He was just pissed off that I was pulling his dame about.' I said to him, 'You didn't, though, did you, min? You haven't been knocking his bird off, min?' And this cunt just laughed at me and said, 'Aye, I have.' I just remember turning my back and walking away towards Stonehaven, catching a lift from a cab a mile down the road. I never went to Newtonhill again.

Anyway, back to the Star and Garter, and this row had pulled a lot of us in. I was challenged and walked away from it, my mate in tow, to calm down and try to work out what I wanted to do. You know how it is when the drink is in you and you're out for a good time, but something happens or someone crosses you and you just want to kick some fucker's head in or smash something. This is when most lads pop a knuckle or break a toe on a wall. It's just blind fury. The best way to deal with it is to take yourself out of the loop, which is what I did, but I was fucking seething with rage and headed up Union Street banging into people. Anyway, my man stepped up beside me and we were stood at C&A going on about what had just happened when we overheard this idiot giving a hard time to his dame, just round the corner at the first bus stop on Bridge Street. My mate shook his head, but I kept watching as the guy got louder and louder.

Now it might well be that this dame deserved the slagging he was giving her, but then he started slapping her face in taunting fashion and jabbing her in the belly. By now the two of us along with a good few other folk had just about had enough of this cunt. He grabbed this dame's face and as she pulled away from him we clocked that she was pregnant, and here was this fucking mug jabbing her in the belly and going at her full pelt. I said to my mate, 'Fuck this, the cunt's getting it severely,' and I made towards him.

What happened next was the best anger-management technique I have ever come across, and I have thought about it many times since to get myself out of a nasty mood. As I broke from my mate's grapple and ducked between a couple of shoppers, a double-decker bus flew round the tight corner. Just as I was about to get the cunt, there was this 'donk' sound as the bus clipped him on the head, and Mr Nasty Fucking Bastard was sparko, flat out on the ground! Everyone round about us was in absolute fucking bits. It was brilliant, and truly magnificent instant karma if ever it was needed.

That was me done; I could not keep it together. As the OB appeared, we shot off with tears pouring down our faces and went to the Belmont and told the story to some of the lads that were in there. By closing time the whole place had been rolling around laughing and the story has been told for many a year!

Although we'd not been involved on this occasion, it wasn't wise to hang around when the OB turned up. If you were a casual, you were always in the frame for getting lifted if something kicked off round about you. So many of us looked like one another that we were all targeted and classed the same way. I've been pulled up for something that had nothing to do with me. On one occasion a Rangers lad had been attacked right in the middle of Union Street. I was at work that day but when I emerged with a denim jacket and jeans and Sambas on I got nicked, because a wifie had given that description. Many times we were herded up when there was the chance of confrontation and put against a wall. Names were taken, pockets searched and so on, but nothing ever came of it. If you were caught in the act of public disorder or causing an affray outright, you would be lifted.

The way of the 'lad' was to box clever. In and out and not get caught. Back off when the sirens were heard or the OB could be seen. You had to play this way. The lads that got carried away with themselves were the lads that got lifted, sometimes week in, week out. Then they were targeted every damn week. They were known to the OB in Aberdeen and in every city that we visited. I was very lucky; that's all I can say. I came close many times. I've been threatened and put against a wall for shooting off my mouth, or wandering out of line in an escort on quite a few occasions. I've also been in a van and let off the hook. I have been ejected from grounds and have had to hide when there were people getting pulled up, but I managed to get away. It was part of the buzz – the near miss or the close call – but nobody wanted to get nicked. Nobody wanted to do the jail for having a day out. I know I certainly didn't, and when the caper started to change, and the OB intelligence grew, a lot of lads fell away from it all. It just wasn't any fun any more and not worth the risk. I am glad I managed to walk away when I did.

Chapter 20

BUILD-UP TO THE
BIG FINALE

THE CASUALS

In the build-up to the 1989 Skol Cup final I had gone back to my roots and spent a lot of time in Stonehaven with a quality crew of mental lads around me. Dependable lads. Old school. Like so many places where I have spent time, there was a good bunch of match-going nutters and I was really looking forward to the big one with them. I guess I could tell that my time as an active member of the ASC was coming to an end. The final felt like it might just be it, and we had a couple of warm-ups to keep the engine greased, as it were, with a game in Dundee in particular that was a bloody good laugh.

A 'light' session had been had in Stoney the night before and we got the train into the city to see what kind of bunch of lads we could muster for a jaunt to the land of the Jute. Outside the rail bar at about 9.30am and there were three or four of us from Stoney, a few lads from Bridge of Don and Danestone and a couple of young lads from the city, as well as the famous 'Blue Cagoule', who was a face from Seaton and a well-known lad. A few boys headed into the big Menzies in the station to buy fags and newspapers, and the rest of us made for the bar. As we entered the bar and cafe area one of the lads got the orders in and the rest headed for the jukebox, which I have to say is one of the best in the city.

The opening tune for the day as the handful of Reds gathered round a pillar was 'You Keep It All In' by The Beautiful South. Grins spread across the faces of the Stonehaven lads as we settled into the flow of the day. Lagers all round and all was well. An hour passed and the Blue Cagoule and I took turns playing The Beautiful South tracks available on the machine, and the group, now numbering between ten and fifteen, took turns in getting the beers in. The Stoney lads and I had played the trump card by firing in the early rounds and now, as the group got bigger and bigger, the rounds were hitting harder money. We knew the score and when it came round to my getting the beer in only a half-dozen boys called in a drink, out of respect, but there was no need. Never let it be said that a Stoney lad doesn't know how to stand his hand or hold his drink. One of the most famous was 'B' from the legendary Sipd, the 'King of Holsten', and a local legend. And the pair of nutters I had with me on that wee mission were part of the same crew. We all used to drink in the same Stoney boozer and any session with that lot was not for the faint-hearted – or shallow-pocketed for that matter!

So the beers flowed and another hour or so ebbed away, and we now had about 25 likely-looking lads in the bar. It was decided that we would get the next train, no matter what. A few lads were ready to cry the effort off, as there were fewer than 50 boys at hand. I have to say that I wasn't best pleased with it myself, but we were there now and there was still a good 40 minutes to the train, so what was the problem? One of my loons was a bit edgy about it, but as the fourth pint hit home on an empty belly I just grabbed his face and said, 'Don't worry, min, watch and see what happens.' It was agreed that a few of the city lads and young boys would take a wee stint around the usual lads' bars in closest proximity to the station to rustle up a few more for the crew. I was glad to say that I wasn't sent out on the hunt.

We'd decided to get the train early enough to allow ourselves a bit of drinking time in the bars near the train station in Dundee before heading up to Dens Park. Another quickie was got in by one of the lads and a head count revealed there were around 40 or so Aberdeen altogether. The Blue Cagoule added that there were a few heading down in cars from the Star and Garter at 2.00pm and that there 'might be a few' on the next train. We all climbed on board the Edinburgh-bound train, most with tickets, although some just refused even after all these years to pay for a journey to Dundee. All of us, though, were up for making the very best of the day despite the weather. It always seemed like a grey day when you went to Dens Park. The north east of Scotland never offered much in the way of bright weather, but when it did, I can tell you, it was the most beautiful place in the land.

Sentiment aside, we were on our way, and to our great delight there were a few 'lads' on the platform at Stonehaven who told us that if there weren't any decent lads on board they were going to fuck it off and spend the day in the boozer, doing the coupons, playing pool and listening to the jukebox as well as the radio blaring out the football. At Montrose and Arbroath we picked up another couple of boys and we arrived in Dundee near enough 50-strong. It was only Dundee on a dour day and, aye, most were saving it for the final, but we needed a day out and here was the opportunity for a bit of a laugh right on our doorstep. The journey time was only an hour or so from Aberdeen.

We emptied out of the carriage, which we had pretty much taken over on our own, and gathered round. There were a few well-known regulars there, and as we shook hands and addressed each other in turn, making sure that everyone was aware of their own even though we had just travelled together, I felt happy enough with our little firm for the day. The Blue Cagoule led the way to the nearest bar, not ten minutes away, and we filtered in to get the beer flowing again. We decided just to see how it all panned out with regard to making an early turn out to Dens. We thought we might just see who came in on the next train and then head up the road. If we'd stayed until near the half-time mark it wouldn't have been the first time that a crew had headed to the football away from home and ended up staying in the boozer!

By now some of us were on the bottles as the earlier pints had taken good effect and gassed us up nicely. If you drank pints you ended up pissing twice as much, which was no use if you intended having a row. It was approaching kick-off time, or at least time to make a move up to the ground, when some sort of din went off outside. The sound of glass smashing came from outside the bar. Some Utility had shown up and given us a wee show. A few of the lads poked their heads out to see what was what. My Stoney lads, dying to get a mark, made to give chase. I knew it would be a waste of time, as the Dundee concerned would be way up near the shopping precinct by now, but I promised that I would go with them the next time it happened.

Not ten fucking minutes later they were back, and as a wee mob of us came out on to the road we saw the last few running off around the corner. I steamed ahead, and as I looked around me I saw that the first two bodies out of the group of about ten behind me belonged to the two nutty bastards I had come to town with. We gave chase right up the road and around the big building into the main precinct. The public had seen us now and I knew that we had blown it for the rest. I was gutted at the lack of foe, considering the effort and the fact that my beer had been interrupted for fuck-all, and as we walked back to where we had come from the sound of the OB could be heard.

We steamed back to the boozer in time to mingle and turn our jackets inside out and swap about. There was no need to get nicked and spoil the piss-up, just because of a load of kids bunging bottles. We finished up as the OB arrived to give us an escort and we were off. We did the usual route, aided by our tour guides for the day, and apart from a few jibes from a group of about 20 or so Dundee youth, who were only giving it because of the safety afforded to them by our escort, there was nothing happening. Inside, we headed to our little pit again. That smell and the routine of swimming in piss were still in place. Lovely.

So we grouped together and had a singsong, bouncing about among our own, and the OB were on us, giving us warnings. It was a right downer. As half-time came and went the numbers were now up to around the 70 mark. I was glad to see that my favourite character out of Tillydrone was among us. The game itself was a bore. I can't even remember the score. I think we won but that was of no importance at the time. The memories of the actual time at Dens Park were all of the OB pulling boys out of the pit and either nicking them or throwing them out of the ground. We had got a singsong together, totally harmless and we knew it, but it was winding them up. The game ended and we steamed outside to the usual early reception from Dundee.

All these years on from my first visit there and the battle

that saw me getting tomatoed, and here were Dundee at it again with their pre-emptive strike, as it were. They threw their first volley and we steamed at them, the Stoney lads right in the thick of it. A few Dundee stood or got caught and we stood again, waiting for the next attack. They came again with more missiles but never ever came close enough to make a go of it. For that we had to chase them down the hill again, and this game of cat and mouse went on all the way down to the road. Here we were met by the OB, who nicked lads on both sides and rounded the rest up on the opposite and furthest side of the road to Dundee. The dogs were out, and as the OB walked up and down the mob, trying to scare us into backing right away, the realisation that that was it started setting in.

After a hold-up of some ten to fifteen minutes, we were on the move again under escort, heading to the station. We were seen pretty much to the station and then the numbers of OB depleted to deal with other business. With only a couple of uniforms on display, Dundee started to show with a few, and we on the opposite side of the tracks got set for a go. About 25 or so Dundee came ahead as we taunted them, and the few OB on our track started to panic and throw warnings at us.

The next moment there were Dundee coming up the steps to the walkway over the rails and we just went for it and steamed in. More Dundee appeared and the whole mob on our platform got into it too. It was a mental little battle, with charges and a few good punches thrown. The poor OB, in small numbers and caught in the middle of the battle, most likely got it too. I would say we had got the better of it and were making to chase them from the station area when more OB and the train arrived. I think a couple of lads got pinched, but the Stonehaven boys and I were OK and settled on the train with handshakes and hugs all round.

It was a good result for ASC and a good day out had been had, in spite of the nursery-rhyme haters. The lads were back in the city by 7.00pm, just in time to catch the happy hours on Windmill Brae. We got off at Stoney to salutes from the boys and headed to our own boozer, where happy hour was every hour! And that was how we warmed up for the big finale in my time with the Aberdeen Soccer Casuals.

Chapter 21

THIRD TIME LUCKY – REVENGE ON THE HUNS!

THE CASUALS

When Aberdeen played Rangers in the Skol Cup final in 1989, we had a number of confrontations with their ICF mob. Now, as far as I'm concerned, the ICF are West Ham's notorious Inter City Firm, and they are attached solely to that club. They have no affiliations with any Scottish club. They are West Ham and England, full stop.

Now, I am aware that Rangers' mob have been known as the HMS – Her Majesty's Service – and that they have an affiliation with an English club in Chelsea, whose mob are the infamous Headhunters. What I do not understand is how the ICF came to be the name used by the Rangers mob at the time of this account. So, from the outset, I want to make it clear that, although I have the greatest respect for the firms mentioned, I do not understand or respect a mob that has to use another firm's name and join up with the English to fight other Scottish mobs! As far as I am concerned, the day's events had nothing to do with West Ham or even Chelsea. The row was with Rangers – end of story.

I had been to Hampden many times, starting in 1982 when we met Rangers in the Scottish Cup final. I can still remember that first cup final buzz as if it happened just yesterday. It will stay with me always. The sick feeling of anticipation and excitement all week and the lack of sleep the night before. Then getting up at the crack of dawn to meet the supporters' bus and all the sticky-eyed Dons fans waiting to get on at the Spider's Web in Dyce. I remember the atmosphere on the bus, the motorway line-up for a piss, and I will never forget that fusion of excitement, beer and cooked food in the Royal Hotel, Bridge of Allan, in Sterling. Wonderful. Then there were the convoys of dozens of coaches and the thousands upon thousands of people getting off them, and the first sight of 20,000 Aberdeen fans, all waving red-and-white flags and scarves. I still get a lump in my throat thinking about it now.

Then there are all the emotions that the game itself invoked. The John Robertson header to put Rangers 1–0 up and that brilliantly executed Alex McLeish curler to make it 1–1. Then Mark McGhee's header to put Aberdeen 2–1 up, and Gordon Strachan, bloody-nosed having been kicked off the park, scoring into an open goal to make it

3–1 to the Dons. Finally, there was a half clearance from the Rangers keeper, which rebounded off the chest of a very young Neale Cooper, giving him all the time in the world to walk up to the line and blast the ball home to complete a sound 4–1 thrashing. I still have my 'Aberdeen Are Magic' flag from that first time at Hampden.

In fact, every cup final day I have been to since 1982 has had its own magic, its own special build-up and its own significance. I have travelled to finals by coach and by train, with groups of lads from all over the city. I must say, though, that I prefer the buzz of a cup final coach trip, and on this day I was privileged to be on a Stonehaven bus full of nutters, including the famous Sipd, who I had lost touch with until that season. In the weeks leading up to the trip there had been a brilliant buzz going on around the city among all the lads. In all our favourite bars, groups of Aberdeen had been meeting to go over their transport arrangements or discussing tickets and, of course, the possibility of a bit of a go with the Rangers boys.

For two years running we had had to watch our team get kicked off the park and cheated out of a result, and that's not sour grapes either. Poor and very questionable refereeing, as well as dodgy player tactics, had put paid to many a good team. But Aberdeen had suffered particularly badly at the hands of the Old Firm in cup competitions. You only have to look at the match at Dens Park against Celtic and the two previous finals at Hampden against Rangers, both of which ended in a 3–2 victory to the Huns. Getting to the actual final had been an achievement in itself. So with that in mind, yes, there had been a huge buzz around the city.

We made our preparations the night before by getting well pissed up and swapping war stories, and having a bit of a singsong down our favoured Stoney boozer, the Lifeboat. A couple of us had been waiting weeks for our exclusive T-shirts, done up in a 'Locomotion'-style design, with a bulldog character wielding a bat and the slogan 'ASC RUN EVERYONE'. Lovely! After the boozer and the umpteenth reassurance that we would not fuck it all up by being late, we headed back to one of the main Stoney lad's places, where I had been a weekend guest for the best part of the season. He and his bird had been top hosts and that night was no exception, but the lady in question was kept well out of the way, as we needed to do the lads' thing ahead of the next day's cup final. The piss flowed freely and the tokers among us did our best to get the skins together the right way in the hope of producing a spliff that wouldn't unfurl like a flag. I was happy, spinning out in my pissed state, as we settled down to talk all the way through *The Warriors* and *The Firm*, stopping the conversation only long enough to cream quotes from the films. At some point we just blacked out, which was just as well as we had a big day ahead of us starting in just a few hours!

Not long later there was a thud, and it went on thudding for some time. As I woke myself up, my head feeling very fucking cloudy indeed, I realised that it wasn't just a dream. It had been four hours or so since I blacked out. I got up to let one of the lads into our pal's flat. There was shit absolutely everywhere in the living room. Empties, cups, ashtrays and the rest. The place was a mess, which was exactly how I felt and the rest of the lads looked, except for the lad that had had the sense to go home. Good morning, it's cup final day! The lukewarm coffee had no effect, so it was a quick top to toe, dressed and out the door for a much-needed livener! The cold air hit us and woke us up a bit, and soon we were banging on the side door of the pub to get in. Lager tops were the order of the day, and our 'alarm clock' got himself a large voddy for good measure. All the Stoney loons were on the tank already, and what a mad bunch they were. I couldn't wait for the day to get under way. There was just enough time for another quick one and then the bus arrived. We were all buzzing nicely now. Everyone had that knowing glint in his eye. This was going to be a top day – the best one yet – I could feel it!

The journey was over in no time at all. There had been a few beers passed round and the card school at the back of the bus had been a source of constant amusement. The buzz all round had been unstoppable, and now we were there in Glasgow once again heading towards Hampden. There had been so many buses and cars full of red and white on the road down that it gave you an overwhelming sense of pride. It was hard to describe. You really have to be bang into your football to understand and appreciate it. People were beeping their horns and waving all over – it was awesome! However, this was Glasgow – By rah way City – and we were surrounded by folk wearing the red, white and blue of Rangers. Most just let us by with a look. Some jeered and whistled and banged on the bus, giving us the V-sign. But we were not bothered; scarfers were of no interest to us. Although we might have been persuaded to jump off the bus and steam into any Rangers trendies, should the opportunity have arisen!

There is a long road that leads to Hampden with a couple of boozers on it, so we all get off there. There were hundreds of Dons fans milling about outside, socialising and enjoying a drink. A group of us decided to make a play for a beer, while the rest went ahead of us. One of the lads went inside and tried to fight his way to the bar to get the drinks in. It was like one of those social club deals inside and the loos were teeming. Gads.

We decided to sup up smart and head up the road to the ground. So far there had been no sign of Rangers' boys in any shape or form. Then, as we were walking on this grassy patch where the touts were selling hats, scarves, badges and flags, we spotted a group of lads about 100 yards away at the top end of the road. There were about 15–20 of them in all, looking like they were having a scout about. One of the lads with us recognised an ICF lad from last year. Buzzing and ready for it to go off, we carried on walking among the throng of Aberdeen supporters until we got close enough to make a move. We were nearly on them when we get sussed. Then all their boys were looking our way, waiting to see what we had. One of the ICF stepped out and taunted us to 'come ahead'.

I looked at my lads from Stonehaven and we just knew

what to do. Four of us were off our mark ahead of the other lads from the bus, who were oblivious to us making a move. We must have covered 50 yards of ground in five seconds flat! A few of the ICF stood still, but most were already backing off as we approached, with more lads from the bus now moving in behind us. There was no need, however. I caught one of them sweet as he broke left of me to do a runner. One of the other four lads with me took off after him with a kick, and another kept running into another ICF lad as he backed off, steaming him to the deck.

As I turned back to get into the last few that were giving it the 'bring it on' gesture, I witnessed pure poetry in motion. Seeing me coming ahead again, the Rangers broke right allowing a clear plant for the main Stonehaven boy, 'B', and me. As my pal ran towards his opposite number, he deftly swapped the can of coke he was holding to the opposite hand and timed the readjusted swing perfectly to catch their best boy with full force and sent him flying. It was beautiful! I kept going and got another lad with a wallop as he made to run away. Buzzed up, we gave each other hugs and pats on the back and laughed that excited, nervous laugh that only chaps in the know will understand.

As we gathered again as a group we approached the top of the road and the turnstiles were straight in front of us. We could see the mounted OB in a line of sorts, separating the Rangers supporters on the right from the Aberdeen. Right behind them were the ICF that we had run, trying to get some numbers together along with the bottle to have a go. We now came across some of the main Aberdeen faces who, like us, had spotted the cluster of Rangers gathered 100 yards away.

The ground outside the turnstiles at Hampden is a treat for missile lovers. As we were taunting them to 'come on then', the stones came over, making the horses nervous. The OB footmen were aware of us and started to make a move towards the Rangers and us. Knowing that the fun was over, we headed into the stadium to join the rest of the Aberdeen mob next to the fence separating us from the Rangers support. There were easily 500-plus of the best boys there. All the old faces – the Tillydrone, the Hazelhead. If you had taken a busload or a train carriage of casuals from every district from Inverurie to Stonehaven and put them all together, you would have come up with our mob on the day. Every one of them nutters! Granted, a lot of lads were only in attendance for the big ones like that day and maybe, if we could get past the OB, Hibs away. But the stakes had just become too high, with regard to the OB intelligence.

But it was in the blood and we were all there in full song, buzzing and proud to be Aberdeen! Anyone who has ever been to Hampden to support Aberdeen will tell you it is quite an emotional experience. As we were rallied by the sea of red and white to the left of us, we filled the air with our song 'Aberdeen Aberdeen, Aberdeen'. The Rangers support returned fire with a burst of their favourite 'no surrender' anthem. The red, white and blue half of the ground all joined in 'with heart in hand and sword and shield, we'll guard old Derry's wall...' By the time they started into the 'King James' bit the volume had doubled. It has always amazed me how fanatical the Huns and Tims are with their sectarian anthems, especially when they use them on Aberdeen who don't give a flying fuck. Maybe some of us are 'prodies' or some might be 'papes', but we are not fucking bigots. There is a great difference between religious belief and bigotry, and neither of them has a place within football, especially on a day like this. All the same, they do carry a nice tune, and we responded by 'baaing' at them and giving them a round of applause for their efforts!

As we chatted among ourselves and cheered the players' names, a couple of beauts on the other side of the fence started to give us face, spitting through the grid at some of the lads. There was an angry roar, and the mob surged forward, punched the fence and spat back at the cunts. There were boys trying to scale the 20-foot fence to get into them and we were all fucking livid. 'Come and have a go, eh? You're a cunting joke, min!' I screamed at one of the ICF twats that stood on the other side of me about two metres back, grinning like a fucking idiot – funny how I never saw that grin through the back of his head as he ran off with his mates after I cracked him. Bastard!

The OB made their way down through the back of the mob of angry Reds and more of them opened the gates near the track in front of us. We knew what to expect; it was time for a show of force. The brave Rangers now had their uniformed back-up and were full of it. The OB moved in about us, growling in Glaswegian drawl that we would get 'fucking nicked, ye casual bastards' if we didn't settle down, and we broke into song in defiance of them and every other bastard in the ground that didn't like us. We chanted 'come on, Rangers' at them, followed by a huge bellowing chorus of 'stand free wherever you may be, we are the famous Aberdeen, we don't give a fuck whoever you may be 'cause we are the famous Aberdeen'.

As we savoured the disorder, I noticed the OB doing their 'duty'. For one of the lads, a very big name in the Aberdeen mob since way back and a favourite character of mine, it was the first of many exits from the ground that afternoon! With the game under way, the Rangers now broke into another one of their 'orange' rants. We just hissed and booed at them and gave them a wee wave. Then they were at it with the Millwall anthem but changing the lyric to 'we are Rangers, super Rangers, no one likes us, we don't care, hate the Celtic, Fenian bastards...' – yet more sectarian shite that has nothing to do with us. My favourite little number out of the mouth of the Hun is the 'sheep-shagging bastards, you're only sheep-shagging bastards'. This was definitely worth a round of applause, and so the whole mob responded gratefully. Well done, Rangers. Very nice! The ref started the usual with Willie Miller, warning him about giving lip. I thought that what the bastard couldn't hack was somebody who knew what he was talking about. This same fucker of a referee helped bury us the previous year in the final.

DAN RIVERS

The Huns attacked and the Dons players gave back as good as they got. It was another dirty, niggling game as was always the case. As they attacked again and missed the chance, the mob swayed a bit, baaing and hissing at the bastards on the other side of the fence again. A few of our little mates from the ICF were walking about the mainly family-occupied enclosure trying to stir up the snipers, but rushed over towards us as Ally McCoist appeared to shove Willie Miller in the back and Rangers somehow got the corner. It seemed obvious what the deal was again with the referee. It was mental being in a swaying, angry mob. There was the odd outcry or burst of swearing but, on the whole, this was concentrated, tense, simmering fury, and you could feel it in the pit of your stomach! I turned to see one of the main faces working his way through a pie. How could he eat at a time like this?

The Huns did their clapping thing once again, and our energies switched back to the game as Johnston headed off the post for Rangers. Then the ball was at the other end and all of a sudden there was a free-kick on the edge of the box. The tension was unbearable. The shot cannoned off the wall and then – goal! Yes! I have never had such a bounce! The whole red-and-white end of the ground went absolutely bananas! This was it; this was the buzz. The whole mob surged forward and we were moshing and swaying about like loons, still bouncing towards the Rangers fence long after everybody else's celebrations had stopped. I love that feeling, I love the mob and I love the team.

THIRD TIME LUCKY – REVENGE ON THE HUNS!

As we chattered madly, still celebrating, someone told me that it was Paul Mason who had scored. He had been excellent all season. The ground now had that same buzzing tension I talked about earlier, with shouting and whistling but no real singing as such. It was like the whole place was just waiting for something else to happen – and then it did! Rangers attacked and Mark Walters sent the ball into the box to McCoist, who held it up backing into Willie Miller and dropped to the floor! Even though Miller had his arms aloft the whole time the bastard referee pointed to the spot! Once again, the Old Firm penalty gig was in full play and the referee's problem with Miller got out of hand. To make matters worse it looked like Alex McLeish was going to get sent off as the livid Aberdeen players protested. Thankfully it was only a yellow card, but the whole Aberdeen support was enraged, and none more so than the 500-plus lads around me!

As Walters stepped up to take the penalty, we were half-watching the Rangers support, hoping that Theo Snelders could make the save. But Walters sent him the wrong way, and as the Rangers support bounced and roared on their goal we clocked 50 or 60 people in our end, not 25 yards away, celebrating with the Huns! Wise up, are they joking? I thought to myself. Bad fucking move, ye bastards. The look on some lads' faces echoed my thoughts as the already fuming mob started to surge towards the Rangers but they were too late. Half of the Stonehaven bus was on them like a swarm and bodies were flying everywhere. As I ran in to do my bit, some Rangers dame was screaming some sort of abuse at us and lashing out. She was soon silenced as well. One of the Stoney loons, wearing an Aberdeen sun hat, was having a field day.

The OB had the gate open now and were frantically trying to pull the Huns out of our grasp, with more OB coming round the track. I looked back to see they were also trying to get in about the bulk of our mob next to the fence in an attempt to quell the angry Reds and spoil our day out once again. The Aberdeen face who was ejected before was once again led out of the ground, only to appear again 20 minutes later! You can't keep a mental Aberdeen Casual down! The OB presence among us finally eased as we calmed down a bit, but they were lined up in force on the track right in front of us, just in case.

Back on the field, Snelders saved the day as the end-to-end action continued, and Mason came close for Aberdeen. A Hun was on the deck and a shout went up to 'dig a hole, ye bastards'. A frustrating second half came to an end as Snelders saved after another dive and another free-kick, with Johnston missing the follow-up. We had to settle for extra-time, which meant the fans got more value for money, but for the players it was a knackering experience. The booing and whistling from both sets of fans continued right up to the end of the first period of extra-time.

Then there was a Rangers player on the deck, making a meal of a fair challenge and the Rangers support went mad. More shouts of 'dig a fucking hole' rang out, once again echoing my own sentiments. Then the long throw came in from Robertson for Aberdeen and Mason thumped Nicholas's lay-off into the back of the net! Yes! You fucking beauty! The mob and all the Aberdeen support went absolutely loopy again. My word, what a fucking mental bounce! We were all over the place. The noise was deafening again. 'Aberdeen, Aberdeen Aberdeen' went the cry, sending the Rangers support into a fury, so they came back at us with that old and unoriginal favourite: 'You're gonna get your fucking heads kicked in!'

The action on the pitch wasn't over. Snelders made a neat save and then Chris Woods kept out an effort from Willem van der Ark as the game went from end to end again. Rangers threw in their usual penalty appeals as they tried to deny us once again. But this was our day, and as the whistle blew for the end of the match we went absolutely bananas! We'd done them at last. Third time lucky, maybe, but we'd done them, and that was all there was to it! We applauded the team, we applauded our own fans and we applauded ourselves. There were hugs, handshakes and pats on the back. We had had a special victory. Our team had won the cup despite the referee and the bad sportsmanship on the park. And off the park we had come to Glasgow in force and done the Rangers to further back up the point that we were still the best mob in the country! As the cup was lifted, one of Aberdeen's main boys wrapped his arm around my neck and we raised our arms aloft to salute our victory.

The players went inside to continue their celebrations, and we headed outside to see if the defeat could drum up a go from the Rangers boys. There was a bit of a stone-throwing battle but very little else. There were too many innocent supporters and OB about to let rip again. Some of the Stoney and I got a chase on the go, but the Hun scattered and that had to be our lot. I knew the rest of the lads would show their mettle if the chance came about. We met the bus at the bottom of the road again and headed for the Granite City buzzing with pride! It had been a good day all round for Aberdeen, and for some of us in particular the sport had been especially good. The journey home was a buzz in itself as we talked about running the ICF and steaming the Rangers in our end. We hailed all our thousands of fellow Reds on their victory path home and looked forward to a long, glistening drop of the magic that was waiting for us in our local Stoney boozer.

Chapter 22

SHORT STORIES

THE CASUALS

There are several other occasions that were significant to the notoriety of the Aberdeen mob and the press coverage they received. Unfortunately I can't remember enough to tell you about them in full, and my notes have long since stopped making any sense! But it would be wrong to record my days with the ASC without at least mentioning these occasions.

IBROX ZULU STYLE

We went to Ibrox in September 1985 as reigning league champions and totally took the piss out of Rangers. We dumped them 3–0 that day but it should have been 5–0, and to rub salt into their wounds they had two players sent off! When the second player went off nearly 10,000 people left the ground early, including their HMS mob. A couple of thousand of those came down to the Broomloan Road to kill the Aberdeen support – and especially us casuals! It was like a scene from *Zulu*, where the Rangers outnumbered us by thousands and were making this constant droning booing sound, like the Zulus in the film, in between the angriest chorus of 'you're gonna get your fucking heads kicked in!' that I had ever heard.

There were mental scenes outside, as hundreds and hundreds of Rangers fans charged straight into Aberdeen as they tried to get out of the ground. Most were just throwing bottles and stones and whatever they could get their hands on. However, hundreds were just baying for blood, because of the severity of the defeat. Aberdeen held well and pushed back, giving a good account of themselves and the full-on fighting went on for a good ten to fifteen minutes. As the OB waded in and started lifting people and the horses arrived to separate the supporters, there were a few breakaway efforts and the missiles continued to rain down on us. Eventually, after the bulk of the Rangers supporters had dispersed from the immediate area, the OB gave us a heavy escort down the road. *The Sunday Post* did a feature the next day including a photo with all the usual suspects in it. They reported that there were 200 Aberdeen Casuals in the escort. More like 300!

GAYFIELD RUMBLED

Who can forget the Arbroath cup deal? We took 250-plus lads down because of the supposed alliance between the laughable Arbroath mob and the Dundee Utility. The town was completely taken over by our lads and loads of places got smashed to bits, including the Wimpy and a boozer, where some of the so-called 'allied opposition force' and a load of local mannies battled with the Aberdeen mob. There was also a slashing. Then, of course, there was a pitch invasion after the Aberdeen mob surged into the fence separating us from the 'allied' mob on the terrace!

ROWS AT TODDERS

We had a few good goes at the back of Pittodrie's South Terrace with both Celtic and Rangers. I remember one time in particular against the Tims when it went right off at the back at half-time. I think a lot of it was down to the number of Tims that used to try to have a piece of the South Terrace. It got more and more every season and finally something just snapped. Aberdeen fans did not want them two fucking rows away from us, blessing us and spitting on us and giving it their sectarian shit all the time.

It was not just Aberdeen Casuals that were involved. There had been liberties taken with normal Aberdeen supporters at the catering hatch and in the toilets. I remember it going off at the hatch a few times, but then I heard about a Celtic fan pissing on an Aberdeen mannie and his boy. That was good enough reason for it to go off and it did. It started with a bunch of lads, who were already at the back using the toilets and getting pies and teas in, shouting on a few more boys and waving at the mob to come up and see. That led to a surge and it kicked right off. A huge mob of Aberdeen steamed up the steps to the back and there was a charging battle going on between the pie stand and the bogs. I went up the wide steps and into the fray of it and looked on to find lads clambering over the seats nearer the back of the Aberdeen section, closest to the away support, to get in about the action.

They charged at us, and then the Aberdeen charged Celtic back again towards the corner section, and a load of Tims got battered in the loos. They threw bottles and all sorts at us, and I remember a sherry bottle smashing off the back wall, right over the big painted section number. Can you believe that shit? A fucking sherry bottle!

There must have been a good couple of hundred involved but there was no room for going ahead as such. We just had to be content with leaning into the sway and hoped that it would break in our favour so that we could start steaming in. I remember a lad – a trainee manager like me and with the same firm – who was a few bodies to the side of me, he just lifted up his feet in the surge and was swept along with the swarm of bodies. It was a crack, but it could have been nasty if anyone had fallen under foot. For sure they would have been crushed. The swaying and charging went on for about a quarter of an hour and the OB tried to restore order, sending lads back to their seats, nicking a few and ejecting the others as well as scores of Celtic. The atmosphere was evil after that and it went off again after the game, although not with the same effect, in the corner behind the away support section of the South Terrace. Punches were thrown, a few charges went ahead and what were left of the missiles were thrown about.

The same sort of thing happened a few times with the Rangers when they came to town. I remember this one time the Huns were taunting us and the whole mob stood up to address the row. Like the game against Celtic there had been little kick-offs up at the back of the South Terrace and near the back of their entrance. The OB had doubled their numbers on the stairwell, providing the thin blue line between the Rangers support and us. I don't know what happened exactly, but suddenly there was a sway from the top of our section of the stand towards the middle where we were sitting. A good few hundred lads were on their feet and making a move to steam across and into the Rangers that were taunting the most. This surge happened a couple of times, and then suddenly we were across the OB barrier and into the Rangers, giving it to the mouths that hadn't managed to do a runner yet. For the most part, they all backed off and ran towards the bottom section of their strip of the South Terrace, towards the bulk of their support in the Beach End.

Order was gathered again, but the sway had moved the

lads a good ten to fifteen feet closer to the foe, and in the charge a load of seats had given way under the weight of the mob. We swayed back over to our own part of the terrace and the OB tried calming it all down, but as the mob got keyed up again the lads were smashing the seats into smaller and smaller bits. All I know is that all around me I could hear the snapping of seats and seat backs and lads were jumping on them doubled up and smashing the already broken bits of seat, into smaller, launchable bits. We charged through again and there were bits of coloured plastic flying at the Hun hordes from all around me as they backed away like frantic again. It just went mental, and I just can't for the life of me remember why. It really could have gone terribly wrong. The OB moved in about us in numbers, holding us back from going at them full pelt and keeping their supporters at bay 50 yards away.

It was an evil storm, and come the end of the game there were hundreds of lads dying to get into the Rangers and there were plenty of them wanting a go back. As the game approached its end we waded up the seats and stairs and tried to steam towards them at the back again and down into their stairs behind the South Stand. There was a bit of a stand-off with the OB as they refused to budge and very little got to happen, although there were lads trying to break through like some mad game of bulldogs charge. There was no way they were going to let us out and at them from the usual gates, so a load of us steamed back into the ground and along the back of the South Terrace to try to get at them via King Street where they had a wall of OB trying to stop us from getting past. As the numbers of Reds multiplied, a chant of 'one, two, three, sway, one, two, three, sway' and 'steam in, steam in' got the lads hyped up, and, with more lads arriving and one final surge, the mob broke free. We steamed through the OB, scattering on to King Street and tearing up towards where the Rangers were dispersing. It really was a mental day!

Chapter 23

THE BEST
OF THE BEST

THE CASUALS

THE BEST BATTLES

There were so many battles with other teams' mobs during the time I was an Aberdeen Casual. So many other firms hated us and wanted to get a result against us. A lot of teams had a crew of sorts and may well have been able to hold their own with smaller mobs but never really fancied taking it to Aberdeen, knowing full well that it would be folly on their part when the end result would see them getting it severely. However, there were a few teams that either had good numbers owing to their scarfer presence, or could muster a decent enough crew of game lads to put on a show against the Aberdeen mob.

So what constitutes the accolade of a 'best' battle? I suppose it would have to be a 'day out' where we came up against a good opposition firm that stood and had a bit of a go or came back at us when we charged at them, or even came at us first. I won't deny the buzz or the satisfaction that you got from a day where you had the foe in your sights and you steamed in to them and sent them packing. Of course, it was a buzz and you were well chuffed at being part of a result. However, it was better, I always felt, if you got into a bit of a to and fro with the other mob and then got the result. For a start off, there was a lot more credibility to it and the buzz was brilliant. The whole danger and adrenalin thing was such a rush. At the peak of it all, mid- to late-80s, there were people quoted in the media saying it was better than sex and shit like that. Now, I didn't like the complications of having to deal with a dame and also having to deal with the football back then. A few of the lads had nagging birds and it seemed to conflict with their day out at some point. I was not into the commitment or responsibilities that came with a steady relationship. I was a young lad and I was into the caper, the crack, the 'fun of it', and the football and the buzz connected with it was plenty enough for me. That was my only commitment really, during my teenage years and into my very early twenties.

YOU'LL NEVER TAKE THE CASUALS – COME ON, CELTIC

So the best battles were always against the mobs that wanted to take it to us. The Old Firm fucking hated us anyway, especially the Celtic supporters. It really was mental back in the early days and some of the most mental battles were against Celtic at Celtic Park. It would usually go off as soon as we came out of the train station and headed to the usual bars. London Road is where we would start to enter Tim mannie territory, and as soon as they had a few together they would come and have a go at us. Likewise, when we've seen them in big clusters and they've beckoned us to come ahead we've gone for it. Early battles there would see them getting off buses in droves and coming out of bars mob-handed, and mad running battles would go off. They always seemed like great, long rows, but I suppose, by the time the OB would turn up, it maybe went ahead for about ten to fifteen minutes at a time, with breakaway efforts and mini skirmishes all the way to and from the ground.

That first cup encounter at Parkhead scared the shit out of me but was one of the most mental and evil atmospheres that I have ever been a part of and the battle in the enclosure was just as mad as it can get. I will never forget the way we wound each other up and then tried to get at each other through the barriers and the line of OB. It really was fucking mental seeing those barriers giving way like they were made of tin foil, all twisted up and buckled, and then seeing all those Celtic steaming towards us and into us. There were hundreds of people caught up in the fighting and it could have gone really nasty indeed. Mad as it may sound, given what I have already said, that was definitely one of the best battles I was a part of.

The battle outside Dens Park in 1987 after being beaten in the cup replay was also a mental battle. Even though I nearly had my chips! Then there was the battle at Pittodrie against Celtic where it kept going off at the back of the terraces. It was very rare that something would ever happen at home and especially in the ground itself. There were cameras of sorts in the ground and with it being an all-seater stadium there was very little room to manoeuvre. Yet on this occasion all hell broke loose. That day was one of the best, if not *the* best, battle I was ever in at Pittodrie.

YOU'RE GONNA GET YOUR FUCKING HEADS KICKED IN – RANGERS' FAVOURITE SONG

Now, I suppose I can't go through this chapter without giving mention to a couple of the best battles with Rangers. For some of the lads the highlight of the season would be the visits to Ibrox or, as a bonus, if we were in the cup final against the Huns, which happened a few times through the decade. I have personally never enjoyed visits to Ibrox. I don't like the ground, the team, the atmosphere or the supporters. You get where I am coming from here? Going to Hampden may have been a hassle, but I preferred my cup final day out on the coach to getting the tube to Govan and the walk to Ibrox Park, which was always a nasty one. There weren't any more Bears roaming around than there were Tims, but I just never got on with it. My own personal experiences of confrontations with Rangers supporters prior to turning trendy had been bad ones, and when I turned trendy they just got more intense.

The first few visits to Rangers by coach had seen us beating the Huns 3–0 with Frank McDougall taking the piss out of them on the park and ASC taking the piss off it. As we came down from the upper tier at the Broomloan, there was already a good battle going on outside. This was my first experience of seeing fighting outside Ibrox and, although there were easily 300 Aberdeen, there looked to be at least double the number of Rangers fans, falling over themselves trying to get into the Aberdeen support. I don't just mean the Aberdeen Casuals; I mean the Aberdeen support. The same had been the case at Hampden two years running. Their indiscriminate violence towards away supporters was one of the things that spurred me on to becoming a casual. I was also fucking sick and tired of feeling unsafe when these fuckers were about. The next time I was there was when they had two men sent off and we humiliated them 3–0 and 10,000 of their supporters tried to put it right, off the pitch. That was pretty mental, I can tell you!

It was a similar story on my next visit. I think the game ended in a draw, and as the Aberdeen mob of some 200-plus came out of Ibrox, it went right fucking off again. I was decked the minute I moved towards the oncoming Hun trendies, as was a pal from Hilton. I know that the fighting was frantic round about me, as I had the shit kicked out of me by a dozen or more lads who were scrambling over each other to put the boot in. I remember being pulled free from it all by a couple of Aberdeen lads as the OB turned up but after that it's all a bit blank. I never went away with Aberdeen to Ibrox after that game.

At home there were often little fights kicking off all over the city when the Hun came to town. Like the Tims, they used to arrive in their thousands and take over everything, taking liberties in their wake. In days of old, Aberdeen folk used to stay in their homes in fear when the animals came to town. After the casual boom the odds started getting evened up, and so whenever the opportunity came about there would be a battle of sorts. The game in 1987 when the seats got smashed and we just went for them was definitely the best battle with Rangers at home.

I did enjoy battling with them outside Hampden after the Skol Cup final in 1987, though, when I would say the scene was at its peak and a mob of between 700 and 800 nutters were on duty. Sure as fuck, there were no Rangers numbers to match us that day, and once again most of the aggro came from their mannies. I missed the 1988 final but was there for the 1989 final and that day out was just brilliant.

CAPITAL CITY SERVICE – RIOTING WITH HIBS

As I have already said, the battles with Hibs are legend. It was always a fucking mental place to go, even before they turned trendy. Stories of battles with their skins and punks wielding maces and baseball bats had filtered through to us young lads when we were thinking of becoming casuals and we would just sit there, shot away by the tales. I got to see first hand what the battles with Hibs were like at the Scottish Cup game in January 1983. Unlike the battles with the Old Firm, where there had been hundreds and hundreds of opposition numbers pouring out of everywhere and fighting in the busy main streets, the battles with Hibs were definite mob-on-mob combat and usually went on in a specific area, away from the public. Full-on fighting between groups of 300 or 400 lads was just par for the course when it came to the confrontations between Aberdeen and Hibs.

So which were the best battles with Hibs? Some of the lads will say that every battle with Hibs was special and some will have their own favourite memory of a day out to Easter Road. There were some major clashes between the Aberdeen Soccer Casuals and Hibs Capital City Service, some of which have been mentioned already. For me, though, that day in March 1985 was a crazy day. Aberdeen Football Club were on their way to winning another league title and the confidence among Aberdeen fans as a whole was amazing. Likewise, the lads felt as confident as the team on the park. A mob of 300-plus lads got on the train and when we arrived in Edinburgh we were ready for anything. I was just one of the crew, following suit and trying to make sure I didn't let anyone down. The possibility of someone cowering or breaking the ranks and running away was unacceptable to these boys. Aberdeen were a unit. We would arrive as a unit and we held and stood and fought as a unit. This was part of what had given the mob such a fearful and notorious reputation – a reputation that had spread throughout the United Kingdom. The crown of Scotland's number-one mob was at stake every time a match day came about.

That day in Edinburgh was another defence of the crown. Some lads may say it was just another day out, but I always saw it as a title decider with the reputation of the Aberdeen mob at stake. There was a mob of some 300 Hibs lads out on parade that day to try to take the title from ASC, and we had a right fucking job on our hands. You just got caught up in the whole thing at the time, never really appreciating the magnitude of what was taking place round about you. You didn't stop to think about personal danger. That day, like so many other important days out with Aberdeen, you just waited for the word and surged forward with the rest. It was what was done and that was that. Either you know and appreciate what I am talking about or you will never understand what we felt.

A lot has been said of that day and most of the focus was upon the Hibs lad who ended up in a bad way after the last charge. I truly believe that , even though the numbers were pretty evenly matched and the Hibs were at home, Aberdeen had the better of the day by far. Of course, I am going to say that, but, when we as a mob have come unstuck or I personally have, I have admitted it.

THE JUTES

So, who else deserves a mention for the best battles? I suppose, even though most of the lads in my time thought they were shit, the Dundee lads always put on some sort of show. Fair enough, in my personal experience, most of this was down to them letting fly with missiles, with bottles being a favourite. A lot of it involved running too. However, they did try to have a go and they deserve a mention for that. The battle down from Dens Park, where they came at us with all the building rubble, was quite mental. There was a lot going on and they put on a good display, but Aberdeen just waded through them and that was that. My best battle at Dundee would have to be my first one, even though I got sparked out after being hit with a tin of tomatoes!

THE BEST DAYS OUT

There are many different things that contribute to a good day out, so it doesn't just mean a good battle. The weather you could never really count on, seeing as it is Scotland we are talking about. But there were other factors, like the importance of the game, the calibre of the foe and the size of the mob you were going away with. It also depended on how much money you had in your pocket. Then there was the buzz around town and the build-up to the game and maybe getting a new garment and having a few drinks with some of the lads to see what the feedback was on the planned day out.

The game at Easter Road against Hibs in 1983 had all the right elements, even though I hadn't actually turned trendy as such by that stage. I got to see a good battle between our lads and the boys that Hibs had out that day, and I loved the coach journey and the whole build-up to the game.

The day out to Motherwell in 1984 was also another very special one. Even though I travelled on a supporters' club bus, all the hallmarks of a good day out were there. The vibe was right, everyone was into it, there was a bit of a singsong, the older fellas were on the tinnies from the off and then there was a stop somewhere in Perth, I think, for a bit of food and socialising with other Dons fans. I loved those sorts of days. Even though I was no longer into wearing club colours all over the place, I was still there to see the team win. A few other lads on the bus who were displaying signs of the new look were, like myself, also aware of the potential trouble that lay ahead. We had heard that there had been a challenge to the Aberdeen Soccer Casuals by a bunch of lads in the Motherwell ranks who called themselves the SS. And we knew about the incident when a bunch of the top Aberdeen lads had gone into the Motherwell end and taunted the Well mob on our last visit.

On this second occasion, as I've said, all hell broke loose, with loads of lads trying to get on to the pitch or into the opposite set of fans and also into the OB. After that chaos the abiding memory is of the game being stopped, which would be a feature of that particular season, and Willie Miller doing his thing to try to calm it all down. The after-match mission of trying to get to the bus in one piece was quite a shitter, I can tell you! Just for the fact that this was the first go with another casual contender in Scotland means it belongs firmly in the 'best day out' category.

A lot of the best days out overall were at cup meetings. Trying to summarise such a long period of time with just a few examples is hard work indeed. There were so many days where a lot of the necessary elements were in place. But, if I had to choose just one after so many years in the fray, I suppose it would be my last day out as an Aberdeen Casual. That special day out, with the famous Sipd and the Stonehaven crew will stay with me for ever. Maybe my memories of the early days, when I was still relatively naive about what I was involved in, are not as full or clear as I would like them to be, even though I took notes from the start, absorbed all the goings-on around me and cut odds and sods out of the papers. I guess I just knew that the whole casual thing would be a big deal. But you take in a lot more as you get older and know what you are looking for.

By the time that Skol Cup final in 1989 I mentioned earlier came about, I had had a go at being a professional gent, working in management within the retail sector. I had also had a go at a long-term relationship and that left me somewhat disillusioned. This was when I came back to the football, knowing full well that this was where my heart had been the whole time. I had something dependable here, that no missus or managerial overseeing fop could ever fuck with. Apart from these wee sidesteps I had always been 100 per cent casual. I dressed and looked casual, I talked casual and everything in my life was about being a casual. Casual was a state of mind. It wasn't something you could pull off if you had no fucking idea. Many tried but came out plastic. It's like a musical ear. You either have it or you're tone deaf. It had stayed with me all those years and, when I had come back to the football after my period in the wilderness, I was more into it than I had ever been and desperate to make up for lost time. I had managed to resume contact with a fair few of the main chaps who had remained in attendance in the staunchest way. So when that day out to Hampden against Rangers in the final of the Skol Cup came about I was raring to go.

When it came to that cup final weekend all the necessary elements were in place. As I said earlier, everyone I knew that was connected with Aberdeen Soccer Casuals, and indeed every Dons fan that I knew otherwise, was buzzing with anticipation. I had had a beer in the city in the week and the lads that I had run into were quietly confident that we would be on for a win on the park and a good go with the Rangers mob off it. We might well have been robbed in the last two Hampden outings at the hands of the Hun, but the game outside had been won by Aberdeen. Everybody prepared in their own way. Some bought new items of clobber and others had a haircut. Back in Stonehaven we were all ready for the big one, and we prepared with a bit of a pre-match piss-up in our favoured boozer on the Friday night. A couple of us had our specially designed ASC T-shirts coming. The beers flowed and an unstoppable night was in full swing when 'B', the top man, turned up with the quality items as promised and the night was complete. We were now well and truly ready for our cup final day out.

There was a full-on after-pub session back at my fine hosts' place, which led to a bunch of us continuing the pissed-up madness and blacking out at some ridiculous hour, leaving the place looking like a bomb had hit it. Our rude awakening and rush to get ready were soon forgotten when we met the welcoming throng of already-on-it head cases that were waiting for us at the boozer. A few liveners later and the sore head was gone. Every one of the lads was looking sharp and ready to rock and roll and, as we boarded the coach looking like the cats that got the cream, you just knew it was going to be a memorable day.

I don't know where my head used to go on those journeys away from home. I can't think that I had anything in particular going on in my brain. I suppose I was just taking in the surroundings and soaking up the energy and the buzz among the lads I was travelling with. I suppose the difference between the regular trips away and a cup final journey is the constant flow of traffic hailing each other for wearing the colours of their club. Cars had scarves lodged in the windows flapping about, and coaches and mini buses had flags in the back window proudly displaying the name of Aberdeen. All the same, the journey was over quickly and suddenly we were in enemy territory again. We stopped at the bottom of a straight route to Hampden Park and hit a mad boozer full of Dons fans and we were on it again, topping up the fuel intake from the last 24 hours.

When we spotted a cluster of Rangers ICF at the top of the road, the essential elements for a top day out were pretty much complete. We went ahead and did the necessary and came out on top. What a touch of satisfaction that gave us all. The rest of the day you already know about. I can't describe to you the mad shit that goes on in your head when you're stood there among a mob of your own, with only a fence separating you from your enemy, knowing that you're in their back yard on cup final day. It is just mental. Every fan, whether they are a 'lad' or not, knows the plethora of emotions that you go through in these sort of fixtures. It is bad enough going through the mill at a league game, especially against the big guns. But a cup final makes the emotional upheaval all the more special.

This day was worth every bit of it and the funny thing was that, even though Mr Sipd may have been giving it the cool, calm and collected routine, eating pies and laughing at the state that some of us were getting into, he fair went off his head when we scored that second goal and the final whistle came. You would think that we, the lads, had won the cup that day. Every one of us was that jubilant to have beaten the enemy at last, third time lucky or not. Every lad that was there made a point of looking among the regulars in the crew to acknowledge them for their attendance and efforts in the season leading up to that day. Some of the top lads made their way round the mob too and I will never forget the way that the day ended inside the ground. The after-match scenario was a bit of a joke but all of the necessary elements had well and truly been fulfilled. On that journey home we were absolutely buzzing. Seeing all those Reds heading back to the Granite City for their own celebrations and the singsongs and chatter among the Stoney nutters, it really was a very special day indeed. It is fitting that this was my last 'day out' with the Aberdeen Soccer Casuals. And it really was the best day out that I ever had.

Chapter 24

TALES FROM THE FOE

THE CASUALS

I thought it would only be right to include some accounts from former foes during the time that I was an Aberdeen Casual in the 1980s. They allow you, the reader, the opportunity to see what some of our Saturday afternoon adversaries thought of us, showing both the fear and respect that the ASC commanded during that time. Every firm in the country that had come ahead with the Aberdeen mob had taken a bad one at some time or another. These accounts, from founder and key members of two of Scotland's active hooligan firms of the time, give credence to the reputation and stature of the Aberdeen Soccer Casuals!

MOTHERWELL SATURDAY SERVICE

This account deals with a meeting between the Motherwell skinhead mob and the Aberdeen Soccer Casuals at Pittodrie in1982.

The first trip to Aberdeen, early in the season, was to be the one which acted as a catalyst in the formation of the Saturday Service. Pittodrie was probably the first to be marked down on fans' fixture lists, providing the opportunity for a full day away with the boys, plenty of bevy from early in the morning and possibly a good rammy somewhere down the line. The usual quota of skins and boot boys made the journey, armed to the teeth with beer and cheap wine, with a few normaloids who were accepted joining in the fun.

Upon entry to the ground, it was clear that some infiltrators were among the throng. Unmistakably dressed with bleached jeans and patterned jumpers, big wedge haircuts and white training shoes, they were dismissed as 'poofs' who would run like the hammers of hell, as soon as they were challenged. Quite the opposite was true; these guys were a different breed of poofs. Even when faced directly, they steadfastly refused to budge, although obviously with a significant police presence, due to the threatening look of a gang of skinheads, there was limited scope for a direct confrontation without being left open to arrest.

The game passed by almost without incident until

DAN RIVERS

Aberdeen scored the winner in the dying moments of the game. The infiltrators rose to acclaim the goal in taunting fashion, which signalled a charge from the Motherwell group. Even though they were heavily outnumbered, the home mob stood their ground, albeit there was nowhere to run, as they were backed up to the side wall. The police eventually restored order but the big wedge haircuts were soon flicked back in to place and the smug looks returned. They knew they had achieved their aim with a few bruises for their troubles, but they had proved they were no poofs. The 'casuals' had been well and truly noticed.

The author of this piece, from the book *Saturday is Service Day*, goes on to talk about the popular tabloid perception that the great rivalry between Aberdeen Soccer Casuals and the Motherwell Saturday Service was down to them both claiming they were the first casual mob in Scotland. This is a common misconception that a lot of the lads were under, I suppose mainly because of the media hype at the time. The author goes on to say: *In truth there was never any debate between the groups. Motherwell's skinhead mob eventually followed suit, almost to a man, along with others attracted to the image, but not because of Aberdeen's direct influence.*

He reaffirms that it was not until the third meeting between the sides in the Premier League at Fir Park in the 1983/84 season that the Motherwell mob had taken on the form of a casual-dressed contingent among their ranks.

Whether they took on the style that the ASC had founded or adopted their own take on the look from other sources, the ghost is well and truly laid to rest regarding the original casual firm in Scotland. The facts speak for themselves. Aberdeen were the first and founding group of football casuals in Scotland.

Further contributions from the Motherwell camp and my fellow author relate to one of the two big meetings between the clubs at Fir Park in that 1983/84 season, which was to bring the full media spotlight upon the casual scene in Scotland. Of the first meeting that season, he goes on to say:

Before kick-off, a mob appeared at the back of the North Terracing, gesticulating to the Motherwell fans at the fence to 'come ahead'. A surge of shaven heads along the terracing saw the two mobs meet level with the corner flag. All hell broke loose, with ordinary punters struggling to get away from the violence, clambering over the perimeter wall and on to the pitch while the gangs stood toe-to-toe slugging it out. The police were slow to react, caught unawares by the invasion of respectable-looking youths. Aberdeen were forced back on their heels by the sheer weight of numbers but again they stood their ground, gaining a grudging respect from their opponents.

He recounts tales of joining up with Aberdeen lads on holiday in Blackpool to fuck the bouncers at a club and also to let rip into some Rangers and Celtic fans who were doing their usual religious politic thing even on fucking holiday. There is also a tale of some of the Aberdeen and Motherwell lads meeting up in Glasgow to enjoy drinks together before heading to a game, as well as other tales of mutual respect.

I am grateful for the contribution from this former opposite number and fellow author. Respect!

A HUN'S TALE

A former Rangers lad, who now lives in South Wales, offered this contribution to me. Rangers have long been seen as the real enemy in terms of the battles between sets of trendies or indeed fans.

With the arrival of the Aberdeen Soccer Casuals, no longer would indiscriminate attacks on fans and harassment be tolerated from anyone, let alone Rangers. And whatever they had to offer on the day in terms of battle numbers got the full ASC treatment. My contributor states:

I fucking hate the sheep: especially the casuals. They turned up at Ibrox in the early part of the 1980s, dressed like poser fannies from the discos in the city, at first in small numbers, about 100 or so, then a season or so later, they would arrive team-handed at 200–300. I have seen them coming into our ground with near the 400 mark and spending the entire game taunting us as much as they could. They didn't give a fuck about anyone. Not the Polis or the fans around them. Aberdeen FC started to take the piss every time they came to Glasgow. Fuck, they took the title off the Taigs in their own back yard in 1980 and had broken their cup duck by giving it to us severely at Hampden in 1982 and then did us again the following year.

I don't admire them. I hate them. They were smug fucking bastards, both the team and the fans, especially now that they had the protection of the casuals. We hated the fucking Aberdeen Casuals more than anyone; even the Taigs. My first proper run-in with them was outside the main stand in season 1983/84. They stuffed us on the park and a load of the Rangers support left the ground early. I was just young but followed on with some of the older orange boys, who said that they were off to fight the casuals.

As soon as we got to the mass body of Rangers fans, I could see bottles being thrown and loads of shouting was going on and the Rangers support were charging towards the ASC, who likewise were charging at us. They didn't give a fuck, they were easily outnumbered, maybe three or four to one, but they kept coming and coming and forced Rangers back on their heels, and as the Polis came in about heavy-handed with the horses and dogs, the sheep gathered against the far wall and waited for their escort, taunting, well buzzing that they had done so well, despite the numbers against them. Fucking sheep-shagging bastards!

DAN RIVERS

This passage was offered on the understanding that in the name of fair play I acknowledged the fact that there were results on both sides over the many years that the ASC and ICF did battle. Many thanks to the ex-ICF lad concerned!

Chapter 25

INDEPENDENT FOOTBALL CASUALS

THE CASUALS

It may seem hard to believe given the history between them, but there is now a collective friendship between a group of lads that used to be active casuals in the 1980s. It is a group that I am proud to be associated with. All of them have been retired from the scene for many, many years now, but they still love their football and like to keep up to speed with the clothes. The group, made up of old-school Aberdeen Soccer Casuals and Motherwell Saturday Service, was formed in 2001, with many lads having knowledge of each other since the fighting days when the ASC and SS clashed. With that history in mind, you might wonder how friendships could be forged. As I understand it, the formation came about when some of the lads got in touch with each other over the internet. Stories were retold and numbers were swapped and a meeting was arranged. Some of the key characters in the respective firms were in attendance that day and a blinding time was had by one and all.

Now, how the group got its name is a matter of dispute. I believe it was down to one of the Motherwell lads being pissed, or anyway I take the word of the man who told me the story. I add at this point, that he is a very big chap! It was while the ex-ASC and SS were making merry that they got into a singsong about each other's clubs and firms, and one of them started a chorus of the Aberdeen anthem 'stand free'. But when he got to the line 'we are the famous Aberdeen' or 'ASC' he forgot the words and came out with 'IFC'. When everyone had stopped laughing they came up with a fitting moniker to go with the initials – and so the Independent Football Casuals were formed.

With a long history behind them, and a love of football, clothes and the hallowed 'mock chop' – a wondrous culinary delight, native to the north east of Scotland, particularly the Aberdeenshire area – the merry band have had several meetings since. Just to let you understand the strength of the bond between them, I will relay some of the IFC tales to date.

There was a meeting arranged to take place in Motherwell to coincide with a game, with the Aberdeen lads being offered the hospitality of the homes of the former SS lads. You will appreciate that we have not been at war with each other in nearly 20 years and most of us now have families. The Aberdeen lads travelled as planned but the game was called off, so the gathering was changed to a knees-up and the group set out on the piss. Their travels took them to Bellshill and they set themselves up in a boozer with plans to go on a pub tour. It was while they were busy tying it on big style that the word came through that the current Motherwell mob had knowledge of the ASC lads being in the area and were on their way to the pub with hammers and other weapons to have a go.

Rather than running or calling an end to the night, the old-school Motherwell SS lads put themselves up front and made it clear that the Aberdeen that were present were guests of the original Motherwell boys, and, if this current crew thought they were going to come ahead with the ASC, they were going to have to go through the SS to do it! Now, let me tell you that none of these lads are little people. Time and life have been quite good to the already huge frames on a few of them, and I can tell you they are a scary bunch of fucking loons. Considering that we are all mannies now and that the combined IFC presence was considerably larger and scarier than the new Motherwell mob, they declined the offer and let the group alone.

That is the sort of friendship that takes years to build up. It is the sort of friendship that I have only ever known out of lads from the football, and it comes out of respect for each other as individuals, as well as for the firms that we were all attached to. None of these lads is actively interested in football violence or the current casual scene in Scotland. Aye, we watch from afar. We love to see our teams have good fortune and still talk about clothes and the like, but the scene as we knew it has gone, and the forming of the IFC has given some of us the opportunity to stay in touch with lads from back then and have regular meetings where we can recount the good old days and get totally wasted. We all have the same interests, and now the same responsibilities, and the more we spend time together, the more we find we have in common.

A similar example of the friendship comes from the return visit of the Motherwell lads to Aberdeen for a fixture. While the crew were making merry before the match itself, word got out that there was a mob of Motherwell drinking in a bar close to the ground. There was to be a party of Aberdeen's current mob to go round and have a pop. The old-school Aberdeen lads on hand that day spoke with one of the main men in the current Aberdeen firm and informed him of who they were. The Motherwell lads were there as guests of original ASC and not to be touched. Nobody wanted any trouble and that was that. The boys had an absolutely blinding session that day, with half the group in attendance going to the game and the other half keeping on it continuously! I hear that the last man collapsed just after 6.30 in the morning and all had sore heads to go with the memories of the weekend.

The next meeting was arranged in Edinburgh to watch the Scotland against Holland match. A tidy group gathered for the session and they set to work on some of the old city bars and headed towards Rose Street, home of many a good drink before kick-offs with Hibs. They ended up in a nightclub watching the game with hundreds of other people and were having a top day out, when suddenly they noticed a group of boys making their way towards where they were standing watching the game. These lads were current Hibs lads but they couldn't fathom who the IFC boys were or how many they might have altogether, so they let it slide. If they had taken a pop, the lads would have all stood together, make no bones about it.

I have had contact with these chaps now for the best part of a year, and have formed a good bond with them all and look forward to future IFC meetings. We are mostly married or parents and are getting on with our lives beyond that mad time two decades ago. It was something we just got caught up in. It was tribal – it was necessary at the time to stand and fight for your own. The scene was about one-upmanship and being number one. It was about who had the best dressers, the best fighters and the best mob. But there was always a great respect between certain Motherwell and Aberdeen lads, as there has been a similar respect between the old-school Hibs lads and Aberdeen. The same could be said for lads from firms all over the United Kingdom and even Europe.

For some of us it has been a difficult job getting on with life outside the caper we all used to love so much, but we have moved on and we are all better people for the experience. Aye, it still goes on today, but, apart from a handful of lads who come out for the big ones, the scene as we knew it is over and the foes of the time are no longer there.

Chapter 26

THE CYBER-TRENDY BOOM

THE CASUALS

Although this book deals primarily with my time as an Aberdeen Soccer Casual in the 1980s, a lot of the insight that I have gained into the current scene came from browsing the internet. Some of the forums I found were invaluable in helping me gain contact with many of the old-school lads from my own firm, as well as lads from the various firms who used to be our adversaries back in the day. I have to admit, though, that the whole cyber thing has been a new one to me. Although I have done a couple of computer courses to get my head round various software applications, up until a couple of years ago my only experience of home PCs was limited to playing games like Manic Miner and Chucky Egg on the

Spectrum! Granted, I did get an 'O' level in Computing, but I never took it any further after leaving school.

It was while I was writing dance music that I first bought a computer, but after the fucking disaster I had with the bastard thing crashing and losing my work, time and time again, I went into a spell of loathing for technology and didn't bother with poxy computers for a while. After a period in the techno wilderness again, I realised that it is the only way to get by in this modern world and that I would need to get on the case if I wished to gather contacts for the book and to see where the land lay. I first started to get into the PC thing properly by hitting the local libraries and cyber cafes, using search engines to scour the worldwide web. In as much as public-access facilities let you enter sites dealing with soccer casuals, I finally got a few links to the places that were of direct use to me. Sadly the ASC site had ceased to function due to 'cyber terrorism'. This was one of the many terms I would come to know over the next year or so.

After working my way through the pages on offer, I found myself on one particular casual-related forum. The administrators on the site were brilliant with me and let me post an ad regarding the book. Over a period of time, I made contact with lads from the old days – some from my own firm and also some of the lads I had done battle with during the casual heyday of the 1980s. I ended up being offered a web page devoted to the book and then an admin post on the site and I haven't looked back since. When I first got into the cyber thing, there was only the one site that I used and communicated on, but there was a lot of sham posting from mainly anonymous guests. When I got the admin post I set to work with my colleague to stop the bollocks wind-ups and bullshit that was being posted. Most of the posts were jibes from various mugs pretending to be from one firm or another in an attempt to get a bite from an opposite number. In truth, most of it was blatantly posted by no-mark bedroom hooligans, with no idea or respect for the etiquette required by people who want to call themselves 'lads' in the scene. There is a lot more to it than giving it the big one, as any old-school football lad will know. And as for hiding behind a computer... I have learned that a lot of people get their kicks by blatantly upsetting people and trying to fuck these forums up.

So we set about making it a members-only forum, and we now have some 500-plus well-behaved members who post their banter. I have to say, though, I was amazed at the whole cyber hoolie thing. Lads were getting on their computers in total anonymity and letting rip with all sorts of slander and challenges. But a lot of lads were using the forums to stay in touch. On closer inspection I realised that a lot of lads knew each other's cover names and were using the forums to rib each other and share all sorts of banter topics. The few fools with loose tongues who spoke about future rows were unanimously shunned by all and sundry on the board. It seems as though the unwritten laws from the street, born of the original culture itself, have been carried over by many lads, into this new casual scene.

My overall experience of the cyber-trendy boom has been very good. There have been some funny moments and some very funny characters revealing their humour on some of these forums. The topics on these boards might cover anything from 'what about the Chelsea versus PSG game?' to 'what about this Northern Soul track?' A lot of it is about football violence, but most is just football related and the lads on the forums that I bother with offer up advice on various member problems and have a much wider respect for each other than anything I was prepared for.

I enjoy my fix, visiting these sites and communicating with lads from all over the place, I really do. There is so much more that I could say and so many examples of funny threads and posts that I could recount, but I am happy just to give you a little insight into it. The reason is that one of the lads on a site that I visit and post on regularly has written a book about these cyber forums. It is a very funny and colourful look at the cyber-trendy culture in all its glory and will be well worth the purchase when it appears.

Chapter 27

THEY NEVER LET YOU GO – A CASUAL'S TALE

THE CASUALS

The following passage was written by a former foe and one of the Independent Football Casuals who I have already talked about. Any lad involved in the casual and football hooligan scene at any time in the last 25 years could have written it. This shows an understanding of the feelings that many a lad has gone through when it came to the confrontation, the adoration and getting your face known. All of this is part of being a 'lad'. Yet, when you don't want it any more, when the fun is gone and when the risks are too high or the 'game' or 'caper' as you know it has changed or lost its appeal, where do you go? And what can you do? Is there such a thing as being allowed to get on with your life?

When you take those first faltering steps into the world of football hooliganism, little do you know just what an effect it will have in your future life. Of course, thoughts of the future are the last thing on your mind as you try to come to terms with the mounting excitement at the prospect of your first real 'off', fighting the pangs of fear bursting through your body, trying to hold the fists steady and not let the nerves show to those around you. As you look around you for the obvious signs of similar insecurities in others in order to calm yourself into thinking you're not the only one who's scared shitless, and none are present 'cause the guys around you have mastered the art of hiding their real emotions from outside scrutiny, the noise of your heart pounding almost drowns out the rising decibels of your mob as your rivals edge ever closer.

'CAAAMM ONNNN' seems to be the buzzword, screamed in an English accent for some strange reason no matter where you hail from. You follow the lead of those directly round you, 'CAAAMM ONNN THEN', you feel instantly at ease with your surroundings, you bounce on your toes just like the others, trying desperately to look like you belong so as not to be singled out. You never think you're putting your future career at risk, or the family you hope eventually to struggle to bring up in comfortable surroundings, the mortgage you might land yourself with and the respect in your own community built up over years of mere survival while trying to do the decent thing by almost

251

everyone you have dealings with. You just never think, it's all about there and then, the here and now is the be-all and end-all of your existence at that time, and that means giving some grief to the bodies lumbering towards you in threatening fashion.

A bottle or brick thuds into the ground a few yards away from you and it's on, everyone around you bounds forward as if the crash of the missile is a signal for the violence to begin. You follow on but hang back a little to size up events unfolding in front of you, but your plan is thwarted by a flying kick at your head from your left-hand side, your reflexes kick in and you instinctively avoid the intended contact, twisting round to deliver a right-handed punch to the body flying past you and landing on his arse. You follow this up with a swift kick to the prostrate figure, which brings forth a howl of pain.

You step back as the pack descends on the fallen foe, rendering him unconscious and away you go in pursuit of another who you've noticed striking out at your best mate a few yards from you. He's clocked you steaming towards him and tries to beat a hasty retreat but you have the scent and there's no escape. You clip his heels and he crashes awkwardly on to the pavement, screaming in pain as his right leg buckles under his body, a swift right-foot volley to his head puts him out of his misery and your whole body's pumping. 'ESS ESS HO-O-O-OLIGANS' the cry goes up as the vanquished slink away and regroup behind the thin blue line that's formed all of a sudden, insults and gestures aimed at you from a safe distance, bravado which wasn't so evident just moments earlier and certainly not in evidence among those being picked up off the floor as you walk backwards with the rest of your lads, laughing mockingly, taking the backslaps and high fives from others in your successful group, plaudits which say you're in there, you've made it, one of the boys, you're a 'lad'.

It doesn't even enter your head that one day these actions will come back to haunt you big time, even though in your eyes you were only doing what young lads do, standing up for your mates and football club, just as your big brother, or cousin or Big Joe next door did when they were your age, taking no shit from larger mobs who think they can take your town or end just by sheer weight of numbers. You take the risk of a beating, or being arrested, you nurse the bruises and pay the fines and move on to the next game and the next target. You go shopping in faraway places in order to find the most exclusive gear which will earn you further kudos from your compatriots, spending money you can't afford in the process but it's necessary to look the part, never thinking that these youthful activities might jeopardise everything you've worked your arse off for over the next 20 years and take you straight back to where you started.

Of course these things don't matter at the time, it's not until the threat of a jail sentence hangs over you that you take stock of what's been going on in your life, like you really are that vicious criminal reported in the local press as being responsible for organising violence on a grand scale. How a mere pub brawl is reported out of all proportion to the true nature of the incident, how a single punch in view of a copper on the way to a football match is somehow infinitely more life threatening than the stab wounds suffered by an innocent drinker in one of the nightspots later that evening and how by simply attending a football match without wearing your club colours attracts the attention of the serious crime squad on an all too frequent basis. The presence of a certain make of jacket on your back marks you down as a mindless thug, a label on your sleeve stands out against the throng, attracting unwanted attention from security staff while you struggle to empty a couple of sachets of sugar into your coffee while balancing a pie in your most threatening pose. The mere hint of rebellion by choosing to stand at inopportune moments during a game is made all the more serious in the eyes of the law by the posture you choose to give maximum exposure to the badge on your chest and the baseball cap worn on top means you forfeit the right to be treated as a human being, indeed the freedom of speech afforded to the rest of this country's population is denied you by virtue of your chosen footwear.

Such is the lot of the convicted soccer hooligan, whether or not they still actively participate in current events is immaterial, they were, therefore they are. The stigma never washes off no matter what good they try to do in later life, be it following a successful career or simply by treating others with respect, that 'name' you've earned for yourself will follow you around unforgiving and pop into your life when you least expect it, causing possibly untold damage. Are you ready for that? Do you really care what can happen in later life because of what you're doing? Is making a name for yourself in 'hooligan' circles really what life's all about? At the time, of course, that's part of it, everyone craves the respect of their peers and once you've earned that the benefits follow. The attention of the local female population, young lads looking up to you, mixing in a better social circle than previously as all your old school pals are cast aside, you are 'the man', one to be feared and respected by all who know you, and even some who don't know you. 'He's a right hard cunt him' feels good when you overhear someone saying that about you, not so good when you find out there's some truth in the old adage 'There's always someone harder round the corner.'

This person of whom I speak is not I, he's a fabrication with a little bit of a factual base. I was never what you could call 'hard' nor would I describe myself as a violent person. I had a bit of bottle but more importantly an overwhelming sense of duty to be loyal to my mates and not let them down when it came to the inevitable scuffles at Motherwell games back in the late 1970s and early- to mid-1980s. It happened everywhere, if we didn't stand we'd never stop running, so we stood, shoulder to shoulder, for seven years at least until I decided I'd had enough, by which time some of my mates had already given up, some had been jailed and I had been warned I was heading the same way unless I changed. The final straw came with the rapidly increasing use of weapons, totally against my personal code of conduct. Feet and fists were fine; cowards used weapons in my book and were infinitely more dangerous than the real hard bastards who I would front without hesitation.

Like I said, this could have been written by anyone involved in the scene, including me. In the end, I felt like I had to get right away or I would have got into big trouble. The scene had changed so much. The level of violence had increased and the use of weapons and extreme tactics on the part of Aberdeen's foes had soured it for a lot of the lads. Then the drug thing happened and as far as I was concerned that was it fucked, good and proper.

The Heysel Stadium disaster and all those other deaths in 1985 were a big wake-up call to a lot of the chaps, and a lot of people fell away from the football because of it. In the case of this lad and his story, incidents like this and the use of weapons in his own battle circle were enough for him to pull out of the scene for good. But even though this chap moved on and tried to get on with his life, when it came to making important career decisions that would shape his future, he fell foul of his own past. His planned career had to be rethought, due to his honesty regarding criminal convictions on an application form, and his efforts at gaining an access qualification for this new career proved to be a waste of time.

His interest in football had been maintained with a career in the amateur game, and his love of his local Premier League football club led him to working on a fanzine. He made plans to get married and then became a father as he got on with his life. An interview, at the behest of a colleague, with a writer doing a piece on Euro '96 for the *Big Issue*, opened the door to his soccer hooligan past now some ten years since finished. It transpired that the writer was fishing around with regard to the possibility of violence at the tournament between English and Scottish casuals, and was duly steered in the direction of a bunch of lads who sent his piece right up the river. The dupe was a short-lived reprieve. The opportunity came about to be involved in a Coca-Cola commercial based around fans from all over the country, including a guy who dressed as a bird at Crystal Palace games.

To cut a long story short, what followed would be a nightmare. After he appeared in the advert, journalists working for the Scottish national press discovered his history and hounded him, his family and friends, putting his three-year-old daughter and future wife through a period of great turmoil. Their angle was that the public had the right to know about his tainted past. He became front-page news as the press ran a 13-year-old story in election week, such was the sensationalism involved. Ten years on from being an active casual and still he could not get on with his life. Despite this, he would go on to make a success of himself, writing a hooligan biography and other football-related publications, and those who had taken the time to get to know him saw the press attack for what it was. This is only one chap's story, but so many other former 'lads' could have a similar tale to tell.

Many people will be asking themselves, 'What has this story got to do with an Aberdeen Casual book?' The simple answer is that this is what any ex-casual could have gone through when trying to put a life together beyond the football casual scene. As I have said, most of us have moved on and are out of the immediate circle of violence associated with the casual scene in our areas and the teams that we follow. Like most of the authors who write within this genre that I have spoken with, I still keep a watch on the casual scene – the clothes, the balance of power and the fortunes of our beloved football clubs. A lot of these authors have advised me that I am now part of the 'inner circle of blame'. Most notably, one of the best-selling authors within British hooligan culture sent me an email congratulating me on my book deal, saying, 'Nice one! Many congrats and welcome to the world of being abused, blamed and criticised.'

The way I see it is this. I have moved right the way along from my days as an Aberdeen Casual. Those days are long gone. I just so happen to have done a lot of things involving youth culture that I feel have been worthy of sharing with others. This book and its contents are just part of those experiences. They are not meant as a boast or an incitement. They are just one lad's observations and simply a reflection of a scene and a movement that has had its own tale to tell within our youth culture.

Chapter 28

AN HONEST VIEW
OF THE BOOK

THE CASUALS

I had no idea how to go about writing this book. I only own three hooligan biographies and two of those are Scottish. The first book I ever purchased on the subject was the original Aberdeen Soccer Casuals book. I have given that work its due respect in different parts of this book. The second of the three I got as part of a deal at HMV, and the publisher of that book is the one I chose to lodge my manuscript with. The third book is the biography of a former foe who I now count as a friend, and is his take on the casual scene in Scotland as part of a rival firm.

The original Aberdeen book I have had for about 15 years. It definitely influenced my decision to write a book from my own point of view. I had written notes on bits of paper and kept diaries for many years during the 1980s, as well as having mental notes in my memory. These are the ones that might get a bit fuzzy sometimes, but they can't be mislaid or destroyed by the process of time. When I tried pulling all the material and ideas together to lay them down in some sort of format, I was conscious that all I had were diary accounts from days out and that it might come across as samey or arrogant. I have been told that many football hooligan books have this element in them. The way I see it, there is no need for shock tactics or over-the-top descriptions of extreme violence, made up or otherwise. If there is genuine truth in what you are writing, then surely the work you produce will come across with a lot more credibility. Not only for yourself as the writer but also for the firm you are writing about.

As I started putting chapter headings together and jotted down ideas in an attempt to mould a cohesive shape from the memories and bits of paper, I will admit that I saw a lot of it as arrogant and cocky – but that is what it was all about back then. As I've said many times, the whole deal was about one-upmanship and being number one, and that is exactly who we were. No doubt about it. History cannot be changed. We were a force to be reckoned with, above all others. Granted, our closest rivals Hibs came into their own at the end of the decade and respect is due to them, but this is a book about Aberdeen. More specifically, it is about casual culture and my time as an Aberdeen Soccer Casual.

DAN RIVERS

It would be so easy to write a book saying how we smashed this mob and took 500 here and there, blah blah blah blah blah. We have a credible enough history to warrant a much bigger book full of those sorts of accounts if it were really necessary. We were always ready for the violence and we were more than capable of giving it out as well as taking it. It was part and parcel of what being an Aberdeen Casual was about. But I reiterate that for me it was about more than just the violence itself. There were so many days out that had no violent incident in them. Sometimes people just didn't fancy trying it on with us, and fair play to them for that. Also, there were times when we travelled to some places and didn't attend the match itself. We just holed up in a boozer somewhere along the way and listened to the game on the radio and played pool and the jukebox all day getting drunk. Those were also brilliant days out. As many a real lad will tell you, it is all about being out with your crew and making a day of it, whether there is violence or not.

Just being part of the Aberdeen mob was the biggest buzz for me. I have been out in the city or away at the likes of Dundee with a group of 20-plus boys in a bar and had a mental time. Likewise I have been in the city at one of our favourite boozers when the likes of Rangers have been in town and there have been 50 to 80 boys on board with 500 to 600 boys weaving about the city looking for the foe and keeping us informed on any developments. The same buzz came from getting on a train team-handed with 300 to 500 nutters, nodding to the dozen or so OB clocking each and every one of you climbing on the hot rails to hoolieville! It was just such a buzz, you know, just mental fun. You know that 'fun of it' factor that I mentioned in the early chapters? That was what it was all about. I never really grasped the seriousness or the magnitude of what I was mixed up in and an active part of. Not until I was on the receiving end of it properly, and even then I was back the next week.

It was not until I took myself out of the loop for a while that it started to sink in. By then, the scene was changing and the challenges were getting tougher and more mental, but the need for the buzz was still there. The Aberdeen Soccer Casuals were groundbreaking nasty boys of youth terrace culture, as well as style gurus for the whole fashion-conscious nation, and I became one of them. Yet, despite the image that they might have conjured up for the layman back then, or for the average man or woman reading a Scottish paper, these lads were not all nasty bastards. Most of them were the finest folk you could ever meet and genuine people. They were far more mindful than mindless, and, although it is no great comfort now, whenever innocent folk got caught up in any melee that we might be involved in, it brought an even worse stain upon us and our beloved football club. But it truly was never intended. Most of us were just in it all for the caper – for the camaraderie and buzz that came from bonding with your own. We were weekend warriors with a common cause. For some it was a way of life. Dressing and acting like a casual wasn't solely related to antics at the football. There was so much more to it than that and I have tried to put across some of the instances and memories that were outside of football so you can see the effect it had on us and, more specifically, me.

So, as I wrote and tried to shape the book, I found that the direction changed a few times. Some chapters were dropped and others were added, and my whole opinion and feeling for the firms I was writing about changed. Yes, I have put across an Aberdeen point of view through my eyes. We were number one and that was how I saw it, but we never had it all our own way all of the time, and I have tried to put that across also. I have also done the right thing and given respect where it was due to those who were our opposite numbers at the time. Sure there is bias, but, as our national comic idol (that's Billy Connelly, of course) relayed once before, it's a disease and you know it. I have it for my team in my neck of the woods and you have it for your team in yours. It is a tribal thing and it spreads itself all across the borders and oceans of the land and pops its head up in battles and confrontations as it has done for centuries. This football-violence culture, as I have said in the book, is only a part of a far bigger picture in gang culture and not nearly as nasty as some of the shit that really does affect innocent folk.

Chapter 29

LOOKING BACK

THE CASUALS

Looking back, my time as an Aberdeen Casual was one of the best and most mental times of my life. I was part of something that shaped youth culture, and I had the best years with the biggest and hardest firm in Scotland. So why did I become a casual? The simple answer is still 'for the fun of it'! I was drawn to it. I loved it – all of it – and I didn't even mind the kickings. My experiences as a casual have shaped a great deal of my life. I still dress and look the part in as much as I can, even though I have been retired for 14 years. I've learned to look after myself because of it. I've also learned the value of loyalty and trust from those days, and I must say I've seldom known loyalty like that shown by the lads at the football. The casual scene was about one-upmanship, but it was still all about being a group. Aye, you had your top boys, which was only right enough. The order of rank was understood and respected, but nobody tried to fuck each other over in our mob. As I saw it, it was about watching each other's back, being willing to put yourself in harm's way to save the boys in your mob, and standing beside them.

Now, 'standing' is the main point here. 'Standing' by your lads and being ready and willing to 'stand' and fight and do the necessary. 'Standing' your ground – not only in battle but 'standing' by the code and 'standing' by your beliefs and your culture! It might all sound like bullshit to the uneducated or non-believers, but anyone, anywhere, that has ever been part of a football crew will know that I am talking the truth. I went into the dance scene after the football and it was bullshit – full of wankers and so-called big men. Maybe if I'd stayed in Aberdeen it might have been different. Saying that, I felt that it was time to pull away and try something different, so I did just that. I think a lot my experiences within the dance scene were soured because of the many cliques and groups of individuals who were out to dominate and fuck other people over within their own scene. I could never get my head round it. There was no code – just greed.

I believe that wherever there are drugs involved people can't be trusted. They alter your perception as a user and inflate your ego as a dealer, even at the lowest level, and sooner or later a fuck-up of sorts is guaranteed. People in the dance scene would block your progress and ambition if you weren't part of the 'in crowd' or shun you if you were in trouble; that never happened within the casual scene. Not in my experience anyway.

Football, fashion and music may move and change but the casual scene embraces the change and goes with it. The fundamental values remain. Right enough, there were serious operators within the scene – the real dressers, the boys that had all the labels, accessories, jewellery and gold. Yet some lads had very little or fuck-all. All of them, however, had the same fundamental beliefs and followed the same code. They were 100 per cent Aberdeen and were willing to 'stand' by their fellow Reds and fight to uphold the famous (or infamous depending on your viewpoint) name of the Aberdeen Soccer Casuals as the number-one firm in the battle of the mobs. Nobody got shunned. You didn't walk away and leave one of your own to get a doing because you were wearing Armani and he wasn't, and like I have already said there were no longer any gang or district rivalries between lads.

The point I'm trying to make is that the dance scene that emerged out of the casual scene at the end of the 1980s carried no such values. Only the staunch have survived and even now there is still a code among the match-going lads. I have had a lot of experiences in my life; some have been good and some not so. The one thing that life has taught me is that regret is far too negative an emotion and too much of a burden to keep carrying around. I have already mentioned the positive things that came out of being a casual, but I certainly don't regret the mistakes – what's done is done, it can't be changed.

As for the battles with the other mobs, well this book couldn't have been written without them and the 'days out' against their boys. We all knew what we were doing on the day and we had some good results against every other firm in Scotland. There have also been a few times when some of us have come unstuck! This is, however, a book about Aberdeen and some of my experiences while I was an Aberdeen Casual. We were number one – no doubt about it. Regardless of how the last 15 years may have changed the scene in Scotland, we were still the first. Therefore, we will always be Scotland's number one!

So how does one end a book like this? I've sat on the skeleton plan for this tribute book for over 14 years. I suppose I was waiting for the right time. The right time, with regard to the casual movement in Scotland, and the right time for me personally. Only since writing this book have I become aware of the current casual scene. It's more than 20 years on from when I first became an Aberdeen Casual and nearly 25 years since the founding of the movement in Scotland, as pioneered by the original members of the Aberdeen firm. Much has changed since that initial conception.

In fact, since I hung up my boots (well, classic old-school trainers anyway) in 1990, pretty much the whole scene has changed. There are still active firms at the same clubs that were part of my days out all those years ago, but things are not done on the grand scale that they once were. The dance scene put paid to a lot of the lads' appetite for the football. It also appears that the powers that be have reached a zero-tolerance level as far as matters of football violence are concerned. The penalties for involvement in match-related 'violent misconduct' and 'public disorder' have become very stiff indeed. Dozens of lads from all the main firms have been jailed or are awaiting sentencing with the expectation of a prison term. No more are there simple fines and warnings. The days of a slap on the wrist are long gone.

Yet, despite this, there is still a casual representation at most clubs in the country. The thing that I was a part of at the beginning has gone through two decades of changing with the times, but it is still there, alive and kicking! The new-school trendies are following on from where we left off and so it all carries on. Some of the old guard are still in attendance but they can't be blamed for the new school or any progressive uprising. No more than books like this can. There will always be a fight for identity, acceptance, recognition and supremacy. There will always be fights over territory, religion, politics and power – in short, one-upmanship. It is human nature. Football hooliganism is only a very small part of the problems within a much bigger picture!

GLOSSARY

THE CASUALS

Bears	Rangers Fans
beauts	not very attractive folk
CCS	Capital City Service (Hibs firm)
dame	female
escort	police chaperone (not the Ford car)
football special	supporters' bus/train
gads	nasty
goodnight nurse	knocked unconscious
Huns	Rangers
Jambos	Hearts
Jutes	people from Dundee
keeners	loose cannons
khazi	toilet

lifted	arrested
loons	lads or lunatics
mannie	30-something guy with a beer belly and a Popeye tattoo
minging	not nice
minkers	cousins of tinks
mooch	scrounge
mucker	friend
OB	Police (Old Bill)
on the lam	in hiding
plastic smelly	fake biker
plastics	fakes
rammy	fight
scarfers	typical football supporters
skins	cigarette papers
smelly	biker
specials	folk that are not quite right
spotters	lookouts keeping an eye out for the opposition mob
SS	Saturday Service (Motherwell mob)
tap	borrow
Tims	Celtic
tinks	scruffs with no idea
toker	dope smoker
trap	pull a dame
Under Fives	Aberdeen's junior mob
Utility	combined Dundee mob